USDA

United States
Department of
Agriculture

Forest Service

Pacific Northwest
Research Station

General Technical
Report
PNW-GTR-746
July 2008

Log Sampling Methods and Software for Stand and Landscape Analyses

Lisa J. Bate, Torolf R. Torgersen, Michael J. Wisdom,
Edward O. Garton, and Shawn C. Clabough

Authors

Lisa J. Bate is a research wildlife biologist, 389 LaBrant Road, Kalispell, MT 59901; **Torolf R. Torgersen** is a research entomologist (emeritus), 4910 Paisley Place, Anacortes, WA 98221; **Michael J. Wisdom** is a research wildlife biologist, U.S. Department of Agriculture, Forest Service, Pacific Northwest Research Station, Forestry and Range Sciences Laboratory, 1401 Gekeler Lane, La Grande, OR 97850; **Edward O. Garton** is a professor, Fish and Wildlife Resources Department, University of Idaho, Moscow, ID 83844; **Shawn C. Clabough** is a software and Web developer, 686 Fairview Drive, Moscow, ID 83843.

Cover

Photos clockwise from top left: American marten in log (by Evelyn Bull); hollow log (by Lisa Bate); salamander on log (by Lisa Bate); early-seral forest with logs (by Lisa Bate).

Abstract

Bate, Lisa J.; Torgersen, Torolf R.; Wisdom, Michael J.; Garton, Edward O.; Clabough, Shawn C. 2008. Log sampling methods and software for stand and landscape analyses. Gen. Tech. Rep. PNW-GTR-746. Portland, OR: U.S. Department of Agriculture, Forest Service, Pacific Northwest Research Station. 93 p.

We describe methods for efficient, accurate sampling of logs at landscape and stand scales to estimate density, total length, cover, volume, and weight. Our methods focus on optimizing the sampling effort by choosing an appropriate sampling method and transect length for specific forest conditions and objectives. Sampling methods include the line-intersect method and the strip-plot method. Which method is better depends on the variable of interest, log quantities, desired precision, and forest conditions. Two statistical options are available. The first requires sampling until a desired precision level is obtained. The second is used to evaluate or monitor areas that have low log abundance compared to values in a land management plan. A minimum of 60 samples usually are sufficient to test for a significant difference between the estimated and targeted parameters. Both sampling methods are compatible with existing snag and large tree sampling methods, thereby improving efficiency by enabling the simultaneous collection of all three components—snags, large trees, and logs—to evaluate wildlife or other resource conditions of interest.

Analysis of log data requires SnagPRO, a user-friendly software application designed for use with our sampling protocols. Default transect lengths are suggested for both English and metric measurement systems, but users may override default values for transect lengths that better meet their specific sampling designs. SnagPRO also analyzes wildlife snag and large tree data.

Keywords: Coarse woody debris, density, down woody material, line intersect, logs, monitoring, percent cover, sampling technique, snag, large tree, SnagPRO, strip plot, total length, volume, weight, wildlife management, wildlife use.

Contents

Introduction

It is the natural fate of standing trees and snags to become part of the wood component on the forest floor. Individual branches, tops, or whole trees are recruited to the forest floor through a variety of natural processes such as lightning, snow, and wind. Other natural processes such as the activity of insects and disease that kill or physically weaken trees likewise contribute dead wood to the forest floor. Insect outbreaks, windstorms, avalanches, floods, and fires can result in large accumulations of downed wood in concentrated areas.

Down woody material (DWM), in the form of natural and cut logs, is a critical resource with multifaceted functions in forested ecosystems. For example, DWM provides a reservoir of minerals, nutrients, and moisture for establishment of tree seedlings (Harmon and others 1986), reduces soil erosion, and contributes to soil productivity (Harvey and others 1987, Jurgensen and others 1997). Fire behavior, management, and smoke production are substantially affected by the abundance, distribution, and size of DWM (Brown 1974, Sandberg and Ottmar 1983, Walstad and others 1990). Many wildlife species depend on logs as habitat (Bartels and others 1985, Bull and others 1997, Franklin and others 1981, Lofroth 1998, Maser and others 1979, Mellen and others 2006). Logs function as a foraging substrate for many wildlife species (Carey and Johnson 1995, Tallmon and Mills 1994, Torgersen and Bull 1995). Other species use logs for thermal and hiding cover (Bull and others 1997, Maser and others 1979). In addition, hollow logs serve as sites for denning, resting, and hibernation for a number of large and small mammals (Bull and others 1997). Thus, dead wood in all its forms is a fundamental feature of healthy forests.

The "life" or persistence of logs, especially large ones, can last several decades or even a century (Bull and others 1997). For both plants and animals, down wood in all forms represents a rich substrate on which to feed and live. Insect-eating, fungus-eating, wood-eating, and predaceous animals find rich and varied sources of food associated with logs. Logs protect wood-dwelling organisms with moist, thermally stable, predator-protected niches. From microscopic protozoa and fungi to birds and small mammals, down wood teems with life. Many of these organisms are connected by functional pathways that are partially or completely unknown.

Logs provide a complex structure where animals find stable temperatures and moisture for nesting, denning, feeding, and food storage. The size (diameter and length) of logs is a key indicator of their use and value to wildlife. Smaller logs benefit small mammals, amphibians, and reptiles, for which they function primarily as escape cover and shelter when the animal can get inside or under the log (Bull and others 1997). Large logs, especially hollow ones, are an especially important structure in forested ecosystems, and their retention has been strongly emphasized (Bull and others 1997, Mellen and others 2006). Marten (*Martes americana*), mink (*Mustela vison*), coyote (*Canis latrans*), bobcat (*Felis rufus*), cougar (*Felis concolor*), and black bear (*Ursus americanus*) all will use hollow logs for denning, hibernation, shelter, and resting. Research on fisher (*Martes pennanti*) suggests that up to three dens may be used in rearing a litter. Although most dens are in cavities high in large living or dead trees, large logs also are used (Powell and Zielinski 1994).

Hollow logs do not develop from solid logs, but instead develop their hollow characteristics as living trees. Live trees that are injured in such a way that their heartwood comes into contact with heartrot fungi (for example, broken branch, broken top, or fire scar), slowly develop heartrot (decay of the heartwood). Once infected, the tree does not die but continues to grow even though portions of the heartwood soften. Over time, the decay may become so extensive that the heartwood falls and internal hollow pockets are formed. Eventually, these hollow trees become snags and then fall over to become hollow logs, a critical resource in forested ecosystems (Bull and others 1997).

Logs in all stages of decay provide foraging opportunities for a variety of wildlife species. During late summer and fall, bears forage on invertebrates in large logs. Bull and others (2001) found that log-associated insects composed a large portion of the diet of black bears. Pileated woodpeckers (*Dryocopus pileatus*) also feed extensively on insects in large logs (Bull and Holthausen 1993, Torgersen and Bull 1995). Most of these logs are in the advanced stages of decay. In addition, *Picoides* woodpeckers will feed on beetle larvae found in sound logs that have recently died.

Small mammal populations are positively associated with cover of logs, which provide not only needed cover but also hypogenous fungi for foraging (Carey and Johnson 1995, Tallmon and Mills 1994). Small mammals also use logs extensively as runways (Hayes and Cross 1987). Logs in or near streams, ponds, or lakes provide structure for amphibians, beaver (*Castor canadensis*), mink, otter (*Lutra canadensis*), and birds and for both passage within and across waterways. In turn, small mammals are prey for reptilian, avian, and mammalian predators (Carey and Johnson 1995). Hence, predators are also associated with log abundance. A study conducted on great gray owls (*Strix nebulosa*) found that prey captures were within 1 m (3 ft) of downed wood 80 percent of the time (Bull and Henjum 1990).

Large numbers of down trees can form a maze of logs, many of which can be 100 cm or more above the ground. Patches of these jackstrawed logs often are found in mature stands and provide critical structure for many animals. Marten, mink, and cougar hunt in them; when snow covers the logs, a complex array of snow-free spaces and runways provide important habitat under the snow for protection and foraging by marten, fisher, and small mammals (Bull and others 1997). In north-central Washington, lynx (*Lynx canadensis*) frequent Englemann spruce/subalpine fir/lodgepole pine (see appendixes for species names) stands with high densities of jackstrawed logs 30 to 122 cm above the ground, which are used for denning and hunting (Koehler and Aubry 1994). Tree squirrels (*Sciurus* spp.) also spend much of the winter in this environment, where they feed on seeds from cached cones.

Logs also serve as sunning and lookout posts. Spruce grouse (*Dendragapus canadensis*) regularly sit on logs, where they apparently are better able to avoid predation (Bull and others 1997). In spring, males use these elevated sites as walkways for their displays.

For fire managers, however, logs can be a resource of concern because of their fire potential. Since the early 1900s, active fire suppression has been a priority in forest management (Norris 1990). This has resulted in high fuel loads across certain landscapes, leading to high-severity fires. Consequently, down wood surveys to estimate log volume or weight often are conducted to determine fire potential (Brown 1974, Fischer 1981) and to assess whether management actions, such as thinning, prescribed burning, or log removal, should occur.

Despite the importance of logs to many resource disciplines, methods for sampling logs have focused almost exclusively on silvicultural or fire applications. Warren and Olsen (1964) first presented line-intersect theory and technique for sampling logging residue in harvested stands. De Vries (1973) later expanded on the theory of line-intersect sampling, finding that given a large number of intersections, this technique could be used to obtain estimates of several log variables. Soon after, Brown (1974) presented the planar-intersect technique. Brown's method was developed to estimate volume and weight of down woody fuels to help resource specialists manage fuels and predict fire behavior. Although termed differently, both the line- and planar-intersect methods have the same theoretical basis and use the same equations (Brown 1974, De Vries 1973).

Line-intersect methods (LIM) were designed primarily to estimate wood volume or weight, but other variables such as cover may be more meaningful for wildlife and other resources. DecAID—a snag, decayed tree, and down wood advisory tool—recommends using percent cover to characterize down wood used by wildlife (Mellen and others 2006). DecAID is designed to help managers evaluate forest conditions and the effects of management on organisms that use snags and down wood.

Log density and length also are important variables that affect wildlife use. Total length of logs, for example, was used to describe the foraging habitat of pileated

Despite the importance of logs to many resource disciplines, methods for sampling logs have focused almost exclusively on silvicultural or fire applications.

woodpeckers (Bull and Holthausen 1993, Torgersen and Bull 1995). Density of logs of specific diameter and length often are used as a guideline for managing wildlife habitat in forest plans (USDA Forest Service 1995). Consequently, given the diverse number of log variables of interest to multiple disciplines, understanding log sampling methods and their strengths and weaknesses is essential to effective use and applications.

The LIM has been shown to be an unbiased method for sampling log volume in tractor- or cable-logged stands (Hazard and Pickford 1978, 1986). It is also an efficient sampling method for estimating total length of logs, percentage of cover (also referred to as percent cover or cover), volume, and weight in areas of relatively high log abundance with normally distributed lengths and diameters (Bate and others 2004). For variables such as log density, however, the strip-plot method (SPM), or area-plot sampling, is more precise and efficient. Furthermore, in areas where logs are scattered and low in abundance, the SPM often yields a more precise estimate with less sampling effort in contrast to LIM. Levels of use by certain guilds of wildlife (for example, woodpecker foraging, squirrel middens) may also be evaluated by using SPM.

Our paper is intended to serve as a guide for log sampling, from the early steps of establishing study sites through field methods and data analyses. Our protocols provide methods to sample logs accurately and efficiently at stand or landscape scales. Methods can be used to conduct research, to monitor compliance with management guidelines or prescriptions, or to monitor the effectiveness of managing logs for wildlife or other resources.

Our methods have particular utility in helping integrate silviculture, fire, wildlife, and soils programs to simultaneously consider all of these resource disciplines in research or management, while maximizing sampling efficiency. Estimates can be considered among all disciplines to evaluate resource tradeoffs and integrate management. Given the small budgets typically available for forest sampling and inventory, use of accurate and efficient methods of sampling logs, such as those described here, provides essential support for research and management of logs and associated resources.

Included are instructions for downloading the SnagPRO software application (Bate and others, in press) for designing surveys and analyzing data. Sampling methods focus on optimizing sampling effort by choosing an appropriate sampling method for the specific conditions encountered in relation to objectives. Sampling methods include LIM, SPM, or a combination. Choice of method will depend on the variables of interest, abundance of logs in the size and condition (decay attributes) of interest, desired precision, and forest conditions. We provide a dichotomous key to help users select the best log sampling method to meet their objectives.

General Information

About SnagPRO

SnagPRO (Version 1.0) software analyzes log abundance based on peer-reviewed, scientific sampling protocols. It was specifically developed to analyze log data following the sampling protocols presented in this report, as well as snag and large-tree sampling protocols developed in a companion publication (Bate and others, in press). Logs can be sampled using one of two sampling methods: (1) the line- or planar-intersect method (Brown 1974, De Vries 1973); or (2) the strip-plot method (Bate and others 2004). In some situations—diverse type and number of logs among strata, for example—it may be more efficient to use a combination of both methods. SnagPRO also provides this option. Log variables include density, total length, cover, volume, and weight. SnagPRO provides estimates of these log characteristics from use of either sampling method, expressed in English or metric units.

SnagPRO allows users to determine the optimal transect length within an area by analyzing a small sample of preliminary data, referred to as a pilot sample. Log abundance and distributions vary considerably across landscapes. Consequently, analysis of pilot samples to optimize sampling design and effort is an important, early step in field sampling.

Identifying the optimal transect length is accomplished by sampling along a standardized transect length composed of eight subsegments. For metric users this is a 100-m transect length divided into eight 12.5-m subsegments. For English users, a 400-ft transect length divided into eight 50-ft subsegments. SnagPRO can then divide transects into four lengths and calculate the mean and variance of each. The length that minimizes the variance—and therefore the sample size required—is considered the optimal transect length.

Resource specialists may customize log surveys to meet their specific needs while adhering to the general protocol suggested here. Default transect lengths can be overridden to meet specific objectives. For simplicity, our paper focuses on default transect lengths. Resource specialists may also use SnagPRO for analyses of snags and trees, based on additional sampling protocols and analysis procedures designed for these structures (Bate and others, in press).

Two statistical options are available for analysis. The first requires sampling until a desired precision is obtained. The second is used for compliance monitoring in areas that have low log abundance compared to values in a land management plan

SnagPRO allows users to determine the optimal transect length within an area by analyzing a small sample of preliminary data, referred to as a pilot sample.

The length that minimizes the variance—and therefore the sample size required—is considered the optimal transect length.

(LMP). With a minimum of 60 samples, users may test for a significant difference between the estimated and targeted parameters.

Files Online

Download SnagPRO from the USDA Forest Service Pacific Northwest (PNW) Web site at http://www.fs.fed.us/pnw/publications/gtr746/index.shtml. The SnagPRO installation requires at least 5 MB of space. SnagPRO requires another 10 to 50 MB of space to operate.

Users may choose where to install SnagPRO, although the default location is in C:\Program Files. Once installed, users may create a shortcut to SnagPRO for their desktops or Quick Launch bar. Once installed, double-click the icon to launch SnagPRO, or launch directly from the executable file, SnagPRO.exe file.

Two Microsoft Excel files—LIMdata.xls and SPMdata.xls—are included in the zipped SnagPRO file. Each file contains multiple worksheets. Three files in the LIMdata.xls and two in the SPMdata.xls contain sample data sets for use with the tutorials found at the end of our paper. One worksheet contains a sample data form that can be printed for use in the field (Field Form). The final worksheet is for resource specialists who want to enter their data directly into a spreadsheet file while in the field (Data Entry). Remember, database users can do the same, but need to format their data as shown in the examples below before importing to SnagPRO. A text file for each method provides the explanations needed for using field forms. These forms can easily be modified for specific sampling needs.

Existing resource data—stored in spreadsheet or database—must be correctly formatted as a comma-separated-value (CSV) file before importing to SnagPRO. For simplicity, our paper addresses only spreadsheet examples, and data files for the tutorial are in spreadsheet format.

Sampling Applications

Our methods and the supporting SnagPRO software were designed to guide the choice of sample design, sampling methods, and types of analyses to produce reliable and efficient results for research or management applications with minimal sampling effort and analysis time. We designed these sampling techniques to address the needs of wildlife resource specialists, but they are also appropriate for other disciplines such as silviculture, fire, and soils. Our techniques may also complement the data collected in other projects (for example, project planning, effects analyses, stand exam, or Forest Inventory Analysis [FIA] data) by converting the data sets to similar units of measurement (e.g., number/ac [number/ha]) to provide additional baseline data for resource specialists.

Recommendations here are based on a log sampling study conducted in mixed-conifer forests within the Columbia River basin (CRB) region, specifically Oregon and Montana (Bate and others 2004). This study investigated the accuracy, precision, and efficiency of the LIM and SPM for sampling log resources important to wildlife.

Methods

Sampling Objectives (Step 1)

Most ecological studies are designed to answer some form of the question: How many are there? For example, do silvicultural practices comply with management guidelines for log density? Or, what is the difference in log cover in areas used for lynx dens compared to areas that are not? Accordingly, the first step in any sampling program is to specify the sampling objective(s). User's objectives ultimately determine the amount of time and resources needed to obtain estimates with a desired level of precision. Objectives can be clarified by answering the following questions:

1. What log sizes (diameter and length) are of interest?
2. Which variables are of interest—density, total length, percentage cover, volume, or weight?
3. Will data be used to check compliance with management guidelines, to establish baseline data for monitoring, or to assess habitat for a threatened or endangered species? This answer often dictates the answers to the following questions.
4. How precise do users need their estimate?
5. Is log species important? If so, why?
6. Are data on wildlife use of logs important (for example, woodpecker foraging, squirrel middens)?

As Krebs (1989) stated, "Not everything that can be measured should be." Time spent on extraneous data collection limits the number of samples and the subsequent results. For example, identifying each log by species seems simple. Yet, species identification can often substantially increase the amount of survey time, especially for inexperienced field crew members. Therefore, users should specify their objectives and how data will be used before starting log surveys.

As a general guideline for acceptable precision, we recommend sampling sufficient to estimate parameters within 20 percent of the true mean, 90 percent of the time. These values are set as defaults in SnagPRO. We have observed that when logs are relatively rare and have clumped distributions, the required sample sizes to gain a higher level of precision (for example, within 10 percent of the true mean, 95 percent of the time) often are cost and area prohibitive. Only when logs are abundant and randomly distributed would higher precision be manageable.

Landscape Definition and Selection (Step 2)

The second step is to define the landscape by delineating the boundaries of the sampling area. Our methods were designed to be compatible with the snag and large tree sampling methods developed by Bate and others (1999a, in press). Methods for sampling snags and large trees were initially developed on landscapes of 1200 to 2800 ha (3,000 to 6,900 ac) (Bull and others 1991). Log sampling methods can also be used on a subwatershed scale with a few modifications. See "Establishing Transects" and "Compare to Target" sections for details.

Subwatersheds in the CRB range from about 160 to 8100 ha (400 to 20,000 ac) (Quigley and others 1996). The sampling area for logs, however, need not be a subwatershed or other large landscape. Our methods may also be used for individual stands (<40 ha or 100 ac), or a group of stands, given that the log size of interest is relatively abundant. If the logs of interest are relatively rare (e.g., <100 to 150/ha) in small stands used as sample units, a complete count may be more appropriate.

Landscape Stratification (Step 3)

Perhaps the most important step is the stratification process. Although the initial investment of time may seem large, appropriate stratification will ultimately reduce sampling effort and increase precision (Krebs 1989). Stratification often can be based on strata established for prior silvicultural or inventory work. For example, many foresters stratify the landscape to conduct stand exams, and their delineations may work well for sampling logs. If log sampling occurs with snag sampling, stratification based on snag abundance is more appropriate. Obtaining precise estimates of snag conditions often is more difficult than for logs, owing to the lower abundance of snags and higher variability of estimates.

The need to stratify the landscape as part of sampling depends on several factors (Cochran 1977):

- Stratification may increase precision of estimates. If, for example, the landscape has distinct areas of high versus low log abundance, establishing corresponding strata of high or low abundance can substantially improve precision and reduce the sampling effort required to obtain the desired precision.

Although the initial investment of time may seem large, appropriate stratification will ultimately reduce sampling effort and increase precision.

- Sampling problems can differ spatially according to forest community type, timber harvest method, or seral stage, and stratification of these conditions can often increase precision.
- Resource specialists may want to obtain separate estimates for management-based subdivisions of the landscape. For example, part of a subwatershed may be managed for timber production and another part may be managed as a research natural area.

If one or more of the above criteria applies to the situation, it would probably be beneficial to stratify. SnagPRO can accommodate up to four strata. If the landscape is homogeneous throughout in regard to log abundance and forest structure, there is probably little to be gained by stratifying.

Stratify the Survey Area

Use the following steps to stratify the survey area:

1. Visit the area first, as landscape patterns become apparent from an initial ground survey. Ask, "What differences and similarities in log abundance and vegetative structure are evident across the landscape?"
2. Obtain reference maps for field use, such as geographic information system (GIS) maps, U.S. Geological Survey (USGS) orthoquad maps, or both. Request metadata (data definitions) for maps and data. Maps should display the following necessary information:
   a. Road system with road type and maintenance level.
   b. Stand or vegetation units and their respective unique numeric identifiers.
   c. Current seral stage of vegetation at 1:31,680, or less.
3. Query databases to obtain the following information about each stand: forest type (low versus high elevation, dry versus moist), management activities, seral stage, disturbance history (wind, fire, insects, and disease) and any other factors that may affect log abundance. Make sure the data report includes types of management activities, such as harvest method used, slash and burn prescriptions, thinning, and management direction for log retention.
4. Check the map and stand data using aerial photographs. Generally, the amount of time spent stratifying the stands in the field is inversely proportional to the quality of the original stand data collected or the quality of the data query. Review the metadata before heading to the field.
5. Revisit the survey area with the field maps. Plan to spend at least one day to validate the information on the map(s) and data report.

6.   Assign each stand to a stratum. Estimate the number of hectares (acres) within each stand or stratum.

Most landscapes targeted for log sampling have undergone some timber harvest. Consequently, depending on the method of harvest, the placement of each stand within a stratum may or may not be straightforward. For example, most unharvested mature/old-growth stands in mixed-conifer forests have an abundance of logs. By contrast, older harvest units that had been clearcut and broadcast burned may have few logs. Finally, more recent clearcuts may have logs uniformly distributed, reflecting policy changes.

For old growth or clearcut harvest situations, combine all unharvested mature/old-growth stands into a single stratum. Then consult silviculturists, query databases, and conduct a ground check to determine when log retention began in harvest units. Place older clearcut stands that had no management guidelines for logs in one stratum, and more recent clearcut areas in another stratum. Generate a new map of all stands categorized as one of three strata: (1) recent clearcut, (2) older clearcut, and (3) unharvested mature/old growth.

Establishing the strata is more time-consuming for areas of selection harvest, especially if GIS stand data are unavailable. In this situation, visit individual stands to examine log abundance and stratify accordingly. Furthermore, unlike the stratification process for snags or large trees, which often can be done quickly by viewing small portions of the stand's edge (Bate and others 1999a), the stratification process for logs typically requires more thorough stand reconnaissance. This is because fuelwood gathering, wind effects, diseases, and insects can dramatically alter the patterns of log abundance along the edge of a stand compared to the interior. Furthermore, both grass and shrub cover near stand edges can obscure smaller logs from sight.

The manner in which a watershed or other landscape is stratified is dictated by the sampling objectives. How does the log size of interest vary in abundance across the sampling area? If the main objective is to obtain density estimates of large (>25 cm [10 in] large-end diameter [LED]) logs, stratification is dictated solely by this LED size class. Stands with high densities should be placed together in one stratum; stands with low densities should be placed in another. If precise estimates of both small and large logs are desired, such as for log sampling to assess fuel loadings (smaller logs) and wildlife habitat (larger logs), stratification should be based on whether small or large size classes of logs are more variable. If snags and trees also are sampled, stratification should be based on the component for which it is considered most difficult to obtain a precise estimate. Usually, this is snags.

Another criterion for landscape stratification is seral stage or method of past timber harvest, which may affect the level of difficulty in conducting the survey. Dense shrub or seedling/sapling densities can make it difficult to sample accurately with the SPM for variables other than log density.

Finally, stratification of landscapes often is dictated by differences in land management use. If separate estimates are needed for areas that are managed for different purposes (for example, riparian areas versus high-production timber areas), stratification based on these different land allocations is needed.

Stand stratification—

Stands, by definition, are homogeneous units and usually should not require stratification. An exception may be large mature or old-growth stands surrounded by stand-regenerating harvests. Trees along the edges of these older stands are more susceptible to blowdown, creating well-defined borders of high log abundance in contrast to interior parts of the stand. In this case, the edge should be treated as its own stratum. Otherwise, the variance within the stand may be so great that it becomes difficult to obtain a precise estimate.

Choosing the Appropriate Sampling Method: LIM, SPM, or Both (Step 4)

The log characteristics to be sampled affect the choice of sampling method. Density is the number of logs per hectare or acre. Total log length is the combined length of logs per unit area (either m/ha or ft/ac). Cover is the percentage of ground covered by logs. This can be calculated by treating each log as a trapezoid and determining what percentage of the ground is covered with these trapezoid-shaped areas. Volume of logs is cubic meters of logs per hectare or cubic feet per acre. Weight is the metric tons of logs per hectare or tons per acre.

The LIM is based on probability sampling (De Vries 1973). To obtain estimates of each variable, specific measurements of intersected logs (diameter and/or length) are taken (fig. 1a). These measurements are then inserted into equations unique to each variable to obtain estimates (De Vries 1973). Only logs whose central axis is intersected by a transect line are measured (Brown 1974). Approximately 100 intersections are needed to obtain a reasonably precise estimate of weight or volume within a given area (Brown, J.K. 1998. Personal communication. Retired research forester, USDA Forest Service Rocky Mountain Research Station). Table 1 describes the log measurements and data required for estimates of each variable using LIM. See formulas in the "Computer Analysis" section for each equation.

By contrast, the SPM is a type of area-plot sampling. "Strip plot" refers to plots that are long and narrow rectangles (Husch and others 1972). Estimates using SPM

The log characteristics to be sampled affect the choice of sampling method.

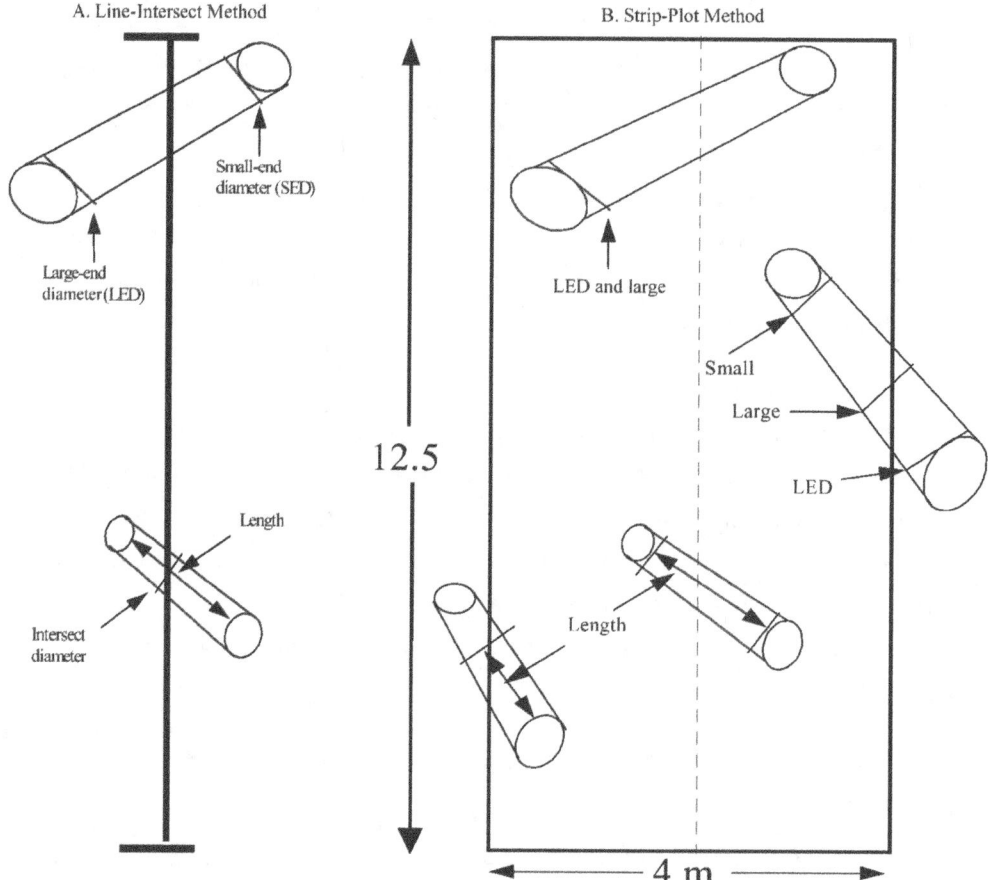

Figure 1—Field measurements necessary to obtain estimates of all log parameters using the LIM (A) and SPM (B). In addition, the condition of each log (sound or rotten) is required to estimate weight.

are obtained by first taking the necessary log measurements within the area of a strip plot (fig.1b and table 1), and then converting this to hectares or acres. For our methods, the default area for a metric strip plot is 50 m^2 (4 m wide by 12.5 m long), centered on a transect line (fig. 1b). For English units, the default area is 600 ft^2 (12 ft wide by 50 ft long), centered on a transect line. Table 1 contains the required information about each log for estimates of each variable when using SPM. See formulas in the "Computer Analysis" section for each equation.

Outer strip-plot boundaries are determined by using a meter- or 3-ft caliper (fig. 2a and 2b) or a customized measuring stick (see appendix 1 for details), which functions as a square. The rectangular shape of the strip plot was selected because rectangles, in contrast to other plot shapes, reduce the sampling variance of logs and other forest structures that often are distributed in clumps (Krebs 1989, Warren and Olsen 1964). A 4-m or 12-ft width was used because this width

Table 1–Field measurements required to obtain estimates of five log variables by using the line-intersect (LIM) or strip-plot (SPM) method[a]

Variable	Field measurement required	
	LIM	**SPM**
Density	Log length	Endpoint (LED) in or out?
Total length	Number of log intersections	Length of log within strip plot
Percent cover	Diameter at intersection	Length, small- and large-end diameters within strip plot
Volume	Diameter at intersection	Length, small- and large-end diameters within strip plot
Weight	Diameter at intersection and condition	Length, small- and large-end diameters within strip plot, and condition

[a] For analysis by size class, the large-end diameter (LED) also needs to be recorded for all variables.

Figure 2—Calipers function as a square when using strip-plot method (A). Two lengths of the calipers denote the outer boundaries of the plot and the place to where the length is measured and the large (or small) diameter is taken (B).

typically is sufficient to sample logs, and is narrow enough to avoid the need for laying out additional plot boundary lines (Bate and others 2004).

The first consideration in choosing a sampling method is the log variables of interest. Table 2 provides general guidelines for the decisionmaking process. For example, if only log density is of interest, the choice is easy: use SPM. It is more precise and takes less than half the time to implement in the field (Bate and others 2004). If variables other than density are desired, then other factors become important.

Second, consider the density of logs present. During the stratification process, an ocular assessment of log density by size class is first done as part of initial site visits. If logs appear to be relatively rare, use SPM. If the logs are so numerous as to be arranged in jackstraw piles and density is not a variable of interest, LIM is preferable. See table 2 for general guidelines.

Third, consider the stand characteristics. Has timber harvest occurred? In unharvested stands, the lengths and diameters of logs intersected when using LIM tend to be normally distributed, with midlength and middiameter logs being the most common logs (Bate and others 2004). In these situations, LIM yields precise and accurate estimates. In some types of harvested stands, however, most logs tend to be short and small in diameter, with few logs present that are long and large in

Table 2–Dichotomous key for selecting initial sampling method within a stratum based on log variables desired

1	Density is the only desired variable; log abundance low to high; unharvested or harvested stands..SPM	
1	Percentage cover, volume, weight, total length of logs; unharvested or harvested stands	2*
1	All variables; unharvested or harvested stands	3*
2	Log abundance High; >11 logs intersected per 100 m of transect .... LIM	
2	Log abundance Moderate; 6-11 logs intersected per 100 m 4	
2	Log abundance Low; <6 logs intersected per 100 m ....SPM	
3	Log abundance High; >11 logs intersected per 100 m of transect .... LIM and SPM Tally	
3	Log abundance Moderate; 6-11 logs intersect per 100 m 5	
3	Log abundance Low; <6 logs intersected per 100 m ....SPM	
4	Stands or landscapes with relatively light ground cover in the form of shrubs or young trees; sampling or travel not likely to be impeded by such ground cover ....SPM	
4	Stands or landscapes with ground cover dominated by shrubs or young trees that will likely impede sampling or travel .... LIM	
5	Stands or landscapes with relatively light ground cover in the form of shrubs or young trees; sampling or travel not likely to be impeded by such ground cover ....SPM	
5	Stands or landscapes with ground cover dominated by shrubs or young trees that will likely impede sampling or travel .... LIM and SPM Tally	

*Users should be aware that in harvested stands composed of mainly short log lengths and small diameters with only a few large logs, the SPM may be a better choice for sampling owing to the high variance associated with LIM sampling in these conditions.

diameter. In this latter situation, it may be difficult to obtain precise estimates with LIM because of the high variance in log characteristics. Consequently, SPM is likely a better choice.

Fourth, consider the landscape conditions. How easy or difficult would it be to travel from one point to another to establish sampling transects? The process of locating and establishing sampling transects takes substantially more time than sampling. This is especially true for landscape analyses. Establishment of transects using SPM takes about one to four times as much time as actual sampling. For LIM, establishment takes about three to six times as long. Although it generally takes less time per unit transect sampled with LIM (obtaining density estimates being the only exception), less information is also collected per unit transect. This translates into larger sample size requirements to obtain desired precision (Bate and others 2004). Therefore, if a large amount of time is anticipated to locate and establish transects, owing to steep terrain or limited access, SPM is the better choice, given that sampling conditions are not hampered by a high abundance of logs or shrub cover.

High shrub cover causes difficult traveling and sampling conditions. In areas where shrubs are so dense that taking measurements of log lengths within the strip-plot boundaries is difficult, LIM is likely a better choice. This is true unless log abundance is too low to obtain a reasonably precise estimate with the LIM or log density is the only variable of interest.

Users are not limited to using SPM or LIM exclusively. There may be cases when doing so results in an unnecessary amount of field effort. For example, in areas of high log abundance with multiple variables of interest, it may be beneficial to use a combination of SPM and LIM (see example I in the "Tutorial" section for details). Use the LIM to estimate total log length, percentage cover, volume, and weight (figs. 3 and 4). Use the SPM to estimate log density from a tally of endpoints of logs within 2 m of the transect line used for LIM (fig. 4). The advantage with this approach is that field observers need not leave the centerline to make measurements in difficult field conditions. The disadvantage is that field assistants need to be trained to sample logs using two methods.

Figure 3—When the line-intersect method is used, diameters of qualifying logs are measured where the transect line intersects the central axis of the log.

The other situation where a combination of the two methods is beneficial is on a landscape that needs to be stratified because of high variability in log density. For example, if density in one area is extremely high, making travel and sampling difficult, LIM is the better method for estimating log volume. In areas that have undergone timber harvest and have low log density, SPM is a better choice. Then, using a special section called Combo within SnagPRO, a stratified estimate of log volume can be obtained. The only unique aspect of this file is that all parameter estimates need to be converted to acres or hectares before this utility is used. See Example 3 in the "Tutorial" section for details.

Just as snags and trees are categorized by their diameter at breast height (d.b.h.), logs are best categorized by their LED.

Classifying logs by size (LED)—
Just as snags and trees are categorized by their diameter at breast height (d.b.h.), logs are best categorized by their LED. For logs with rootwads intact, the LED is equivalent to the d.b.h. if the tree had remained standing (fig. 5). For logs with no

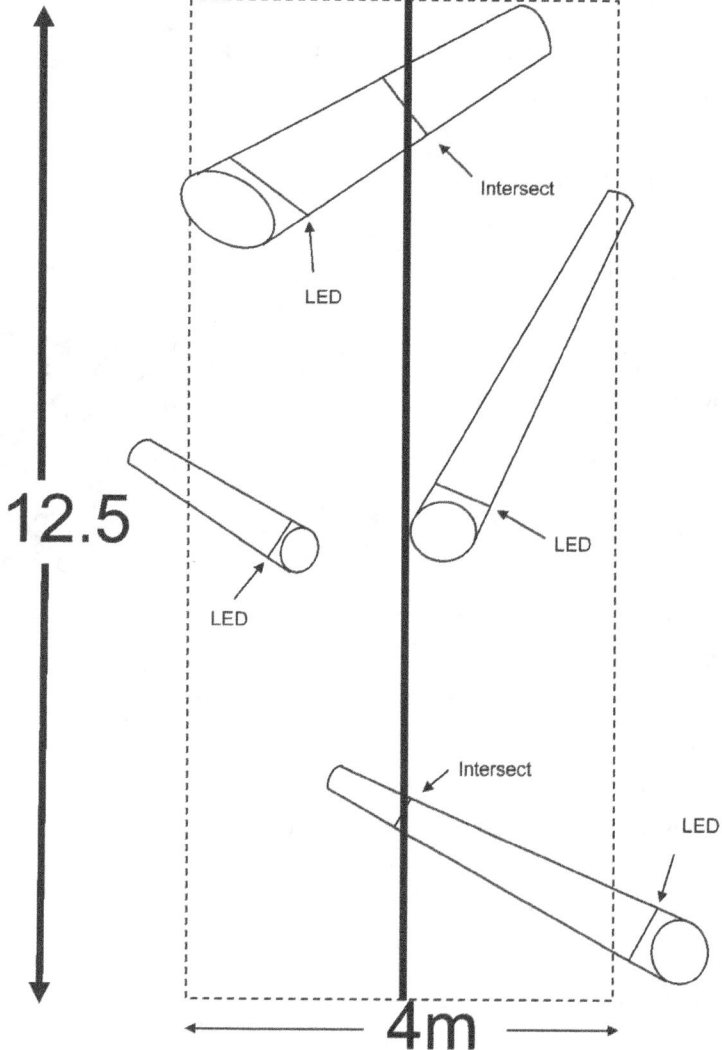

Figure 4—Combination of log sampling techniques: Line-intersect method (LIM) and strip-plot method (SPM) tally. Two logs qualify for the LIM because their central axes are intersected by the central transect line. Three logs qualify for the the SPM tally because their LEDs lie within 2 m of the central transect line.

rootwad attached, the LED is the diameter at the largest end of the log that is complete (fig. 5).

Large-end diameters define a log population and allow for accurate temporal and spatial comparisons of logs among size classes. In the past, most log sampling techniques required data only on the diameter of a log at the point of intersection. This greatly limited the value of the data for wildlife specialists, because often only the larger logs are of interest. For example, two stands may have the same volume of logs. What cannot be determined, unless LED is recorded, is whether logs are small and numerous or large and uncommon. Furthermore, setting a high minimum diameter for logs to be included during line-intercept sampling can lead to a negative bias in the variable estimate (L. Bate, unpublished data). For example, if only logs are sampled whose diameter at intersection is >25 cm (10 in), log volume will be underestimated. How much the log volume will be underestimated cannot be determined; it is a function of the log sizes present.

Categorical versus continuous data—
Logs can be classified by their LEDs either categorically or continuously. There are advantages and disadvantages to both approaches. For research purposes, continuous data are probably best. Continuous data can be used to evaluate, for example, the relation between wildlife abundance and increasing log size. The advantage is that queries can then be run encompassing all logs or just certain size classes of logs, and thresholds, if any, may be detected. The disadvantage is that collecting continuous data takes more field time because the LED of all logs must be measured.

The alternative is to collect data categorically. The advantage is that the sampling is greatly simplified and saves time. For example, if only two size categories are used, field observers can quickly calibrate their eye to the two size classes and leave the line only to measure borderline cases. The disadvantage is that all future queries are limited to these two size classes. For low-budget monitoring surveys, however, categorical data may be appropriate and will save time and resources.

Conducting a pilot survey is one of the most critical steps of log sampling.

Establishing Transects (Step 5)

Conducting a pilot survey is one of the most critical steps of log sampling. A pilot survey meets two objectives: collecting preliminary data by which to identify the optimal plot length, and obtaining an estimate of the total number of samples required to meet objectives.

Recognize that pilot data are not extraneous data that users discard. Rather, they are the first samples collected, and are included in the variable estimates for the entire sampling area. In areas where log abundance is high, the pilot survey may provide an adequate number of samples to meet objectives.

By contrast, in areas where log abundance is low, analyzing the pilot data to determine the optimal plot length can greatly reduce the number of samples needed to obtain desired precision. Use the optimal plot length to collect remaining data needed.

Our log sampling methods are compatible with methods for snag and large tree sampling, improving the efficiency of fieldwork (Bate and others 1999a, 1999b, in press). The snag and large tree sampling protocol recommended 200-m (or 800-ft) transects within each stand on stratified landscapes; however, we now recommend splitting the 200-m (800-ft) transect into two 100-m-(or 400-ft)-long transects (Bate and others, in press).

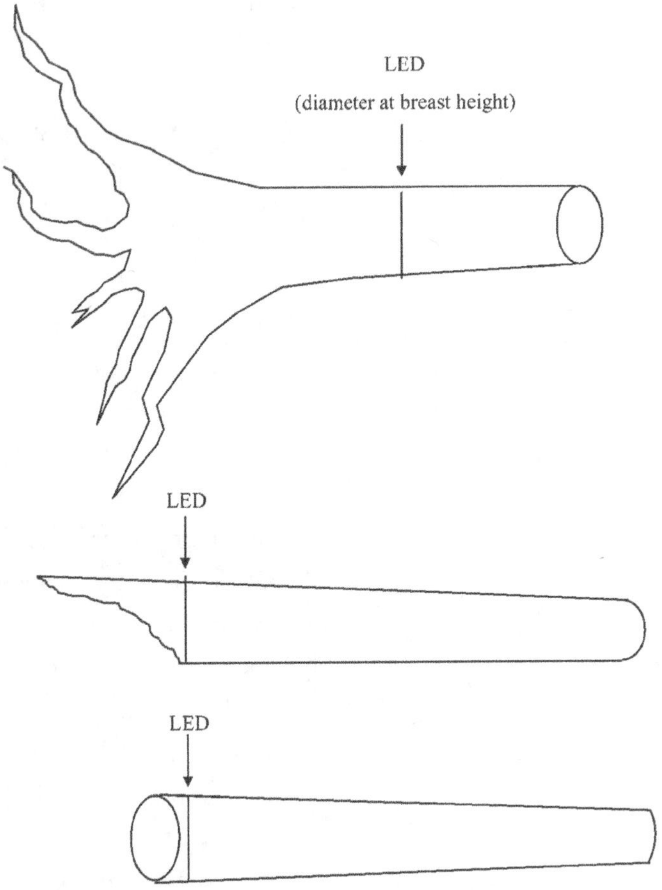

These two smaller transects capture more of the variability occurring in a single stand. Subdivide each transect into smaller increments, called subsegments, to sample for the three habitat components—snags, large trees, and logs. This standardizes the sampling protocol and allows SnagPRO to determine the optimal transect length for each habitat variable based on forest conditions.

LED
(diameter at breast height)

LED

LED

Figure 5—Location of large-end diameter (LED) on log with (a) rootwad retained, (b) naturally broken log, and (c) cut log.

There are two options for locating transects: the single-stratum landscape method, and the stratified method.

For the single-stratum landscape method, follow these steps to establish transects within a single stand or a nonstratified landscape:

1. Randomly place a grid over the area.
2. Randomly select 10 grid points for sampling.
3. Randomly select compass bearings for each of the 10 transect starting points.

For the stratified method on heterogeneous landscapes composed of numerous stands or units, it may be more efficient to randomly select stands for sampling. To do this:

1. Select stands for sampling by randomly picking stand unit numbers from the complete list of stands within that stratum.
2. Place a grid over the stand.
3. Randomly pick two grid points within each stand.
4. Randomly pick compass bearing for each point.

Use a random number generator or table for either method, or generate random numbers for compass bearings by using the second hand of a watch. If a watch is used to generate random starting direction, multiply the number of seconds (60) by six to obtain random numbers from 6 to 360 that can be used as compass bearings for the starting point.

For both methods described above, GIS can be used to map and randomly locate grid points or stands for sampling. The locations of the sample points can be expressed in the universal transverse meridian system (UTM) coordinates, and a global positioning system (GPS) unit used to find these points in the field.

In steep stands, where logs have fallen mostly down slope, sampling biases can occur if transects are established improperly (Bell and others 1996). For example, a single transect established parallel to the fallen trees on a slope may result in a negative bias of log estimates. By contrast, if the transect runs perpendicular to most logs, overestimation may occur because of increased intersections with logs. There are several ways to avoid this problem. Typically, random orientation of transects eliminates biases otherwise created by terrain with steeper slopes (Bate and others 2004). Within a single steep stand it may be best to randomly establish transects at a 45-degree angle to the predominant orientation of the logs. The third method is to establish paired transects within this stand that are oriented perpendicular to each other (See example I or II in the "Tutorial" section for more detail).

The pilot survey should include:

- A minimum of 10 transects, each 100-m (metric users) or eight to ten 400-ft (English users) long transects, within each stratum (fig. 6).
- A minimum of two transects per stand (fig. 6) to ensure that variability in each stand and stratum is adequately represented, providing a better estimate of the sample size required to meet objectives.

On larger subwatersheds, the stands in the pilot survey should not be close to one another, especially for subwatersheds encompassing several plant communities owing to an elevational gradient. In this situation, divide the subwatershed into three sections and equally divide samples throughout these sections (fig. 6).

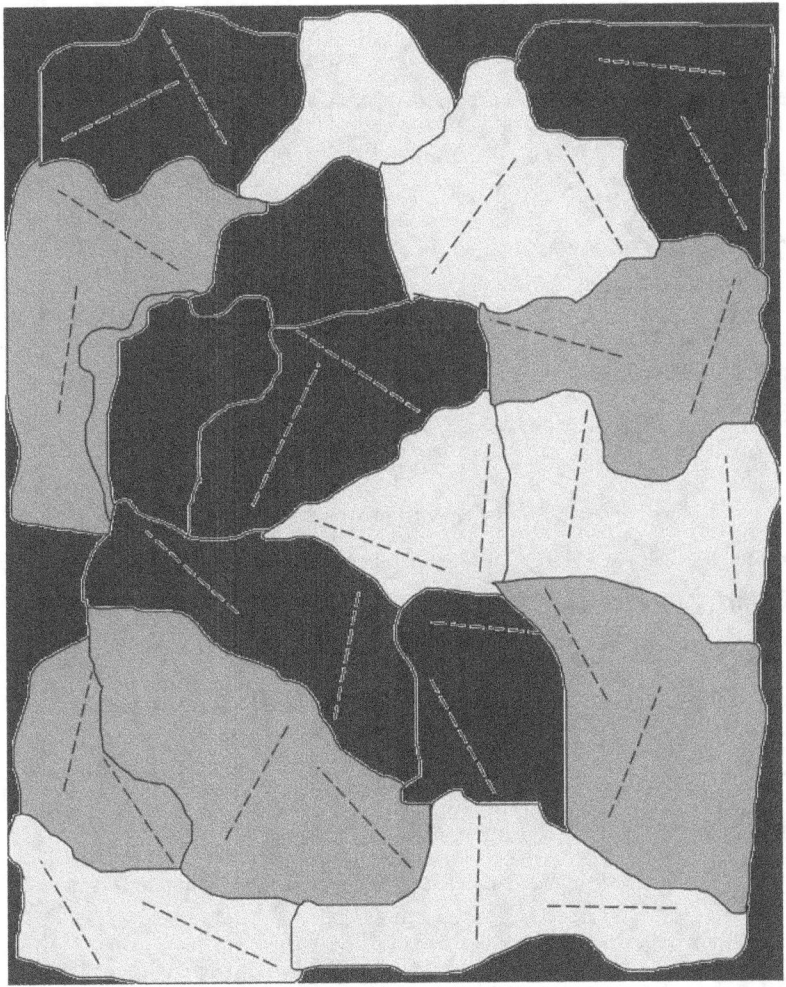

Figure 6—Example of transect establishment for log pilot survey on landscape with three strata. Five stands within each stratum should be selected. Within each stand, two 100-m or 400-ft transects are established. Each transect within the entire landscape is given a unique numeric identifier and is divided into eight 12.5-m or 50-ft-long subsegments. Subsegments are numbered from 1 to 8 on each transect.

Field Techniques (Step 6)

Equipment—

Sampling requires some or all of the following field equipment, summarized in table 3. Where shrub cover is thick, the 50-m (metric users) or 100- or 200-ft (English users) fiberglass surveyor's tape (with a logger's nail taped to one end) is very efficient for marking the center transect line. While one person makes all measurements, the second person ensures quality control (all qualifying logs are counted and calipers are held correctly) and records data. Once sampling is complete, the observers simply pull and release the tape. It slides easily through the thick brush, eliminating a return to the start of the transect.

SnagPRO's standardized field forms include the necessary log information for all analyses. For simultaneous data collection (snags, trees, logs), record the data in separate files. Users may choose to add additional columns on the field forms for a specific survey, but should not include these data when they are saved as a CSV file, or the import to SnagPRO will fail.

Table 3—Field equipment log surveyors may require

Item	Use
Accurate map of stand units or vegetation cover types	Record correct stratum number
Road map	Determine location and access
Aerial photographs	Determine stratum and locations
Orthophoto quads	Determine stratum and locations
Field data forms (hard or electronic)	Record survey information
Engineer's surveyor tape (50 m or 100 or 200 ft long)	Measure transect distances; mark center line
Logger's tape	Measure log lengths
Calipers[a]	Measure diameter and length of logs and boundaries of strip plot
Log measuring stick[b]	Same as above
Compass	Determine bearings
Meter tape >66 ft (20 m) long	Measure perpendicular distances from the centerline
Pocket knife	Determine species and decay class of logs
Flagging	Mark ends of subsegments, if necessary

[a] Calipers that measure up to 80 cm are 1 m long. English users should use 3-ft calipers.
[b] Refer to appendix 1 for details on creating your own log-measuring stick.

We find hand-held computers useful for fieldwork, and SnagPRO was designed with this in mind. Users can eliminate entering the data twice by copying the **Data Entry** worksheet from either the **LIMdata.xls** or the **SPMdata.xls** files.

If hand-held computers are not used, create blank field forms from the **Field Form** worksheet found within the same Excel[1] file by using the following steps: (1) open either the **LIMdata.xls** or the **SPMdata.xls** file; (2) highlight entire page that has gridlines; and (3) choose **Selection**, instead of **Sheet**, under the **Print** options for a form with gridlines.

Appendixes 2 and 3 provide detailed explanations for the correct input of log information using the LIM or SPM. Copy this page to a new file and customize it for your fieldwork. Customizing options include:

- Defining "What is a log?"
- Defining decay or condition classes for logs.
- Defining log size classes.
- Recording wildlife signs.

Perhaps the most difficult challenge in the field is answering the question "What is a log?"

Perhaps the most difficult challenge in the field is answering the question "What is a log?" Clarifying which logs should be sampled will simplify and standardize the sampling process. A log qualifies for sampling with both the LIM and SPM in most studies if it meets stipulated criteria:

- Its LED is ≥ minimum diameter specified by user.
- Its intersect diameter (LIM only) is ≥ minimum diameter specified by user.
- Its length is ≥ the minimum length specified by user.
- Its central axis lies above the ground (Brown 1974).
- If broken and the pieces are not touching, logs are tallied separately.
- If suspended, it has an angle <45 degrees with the ground (Brown 1974).
- Dead stems attached to a live tree are not counted (Brown 1974).
- Multiple branches attached to dead trees or shrubs are each tallied separately (Brown 1974).

For soils or amphibian studies, however, logs whose central axis lies below the ground may be included too, depending on objectives. The objectives of the study will dictate this. Generally, only the portion of the log that lies above ground (central axis) is measured. This situation is common in stands with logs in advanced stages of decay. Appendix 2 provides an example of a definition of a log for LIM studies. Appendix 3 provides an example for SPM studies.

---

[1] Use of trade or firm names is for reader information and does not imply endorsement by the U.S. Department of Agriculture of any product or service.

Log survey techniques—

Conduct the pilot survey to determine the optimal transect length with these steps:

1. Use an engineer's surveying or measuring tape to establish transects, starting each transect from the randomly selected points (described above). Ensure that the transect line is straight, taut, and firmly anchored at both ends.

2. Assign a unique number (for example, 1, 2, 3, . . . etc.) to each transect, delineating the subsegment lengths (12.5 m [or 50 ft]) as users walk along the transect (100 m or 400 ft).

3. Number each transect's subsegments 1 through 8.

4. Measure the appropriate attributes (table 1) of all qualifying logs intersected by the center transect line (LIM users) or of logs, or portions of logs, contained within the strip-plot boundaries, using the tape as centerline.

For studies using only one transect length as segments (25-m or 100-ft lengths), it is still necessary to assign a transect and subsegment (12.5-m or 50-ft length) number to each length and keep track of the smallest increments (subsegments). SnagPRO allows users to indicate that only segment lengths are to be analyzed.

Occasionally, the transect will continue outside the boundary of the sampling area. Use the "bounce-back" method to keep the transect within the stand. The bounce-back method is similar to hitting a billiards ball or racketball against a side-wall, and having it travel away from the wall at the same angle, but in the opposite direction. In the sample area, determine the angle at which the transect hits the edge, then use this same angle to continue back into the sample area (fig. 7). If the transect intersects the edge at an angle of 90 degrees (perpendicular to the edge), the bounce-back angle also is 90 degrees (parallel to transect), but is established at a distance of 100 m or 400 ft away from the initial intersection. This technique allows resource specialists to determine the optimal length and to sample along the edges of a stand.

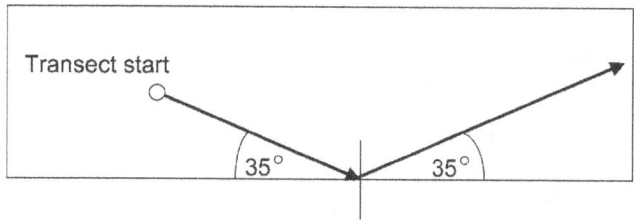

Figure 7—Illustration of randomly oriented transect hitting the edge and "bouncing" back within sampling area. This ensures edges are included in the sampling population while maintaining the option to analyze data for the optimal transect length.

Data collection—

The following are mandatory fields users must enter for SnagPRO to operate correctly when all variables are of interest (figs. 8 and 9). Refer to appendixes 2 and 3 for details about each field variable.

Stratum	Location	Transect	Subsegment	Species	Intersect	LED	Condition	(Length)	Qualify	Tally 1	Tally 2	Tally 3	Tally 4
1	709	1	1			9999				0			
1	709	1	2	9	21	27	2			0			
1	709	1	3			9999				0			
1	709	1	4	9	18	30	2			1			
1	709	1	4	9	20	20	2						
1	709	1	5			9999				2			
1	709	1	6			9999				0			
1	709	1	7	5	20	24	1			1			
1	709	1	8			9999				0			
1	709	2	1			9999				0			
1	709	2	2			9999				0			
1	709	2	3			9999				0			
1	709	2	4	9	19	21	2			2			
1	709	2	5			9999				0			
1	709	2	6			9999				0			
1	709	2	7	3	8	20	1			2			
1	709	2	7	3	22	22	1						
1	709	2	8			9999				3			
1	709	3	1			9999				0			
1	709	3	2	6	33	31	2			0			
1	709	3	3			9999				0			
1	709	3	4			9999				2			
1	709	3	5	3	13	22	1			0			
1	709	3	6	3	12	25	1			1			
1	709	3	7	1	10	20	2			2			
1	709	3	8	3	21	26	2			2			
1	709	3	8	1	23	24	1			4			
1	709	3	8	3	33	46	1						
1	709	4	1	5	16	21	2			2			

Figure 8—Example of correct formatting and column placement of line-intersect method (LIM) data before importing into SnagPRO. All columns would be filled only if all variables were measured. Each beginning subsegment on a transect is given the number "1." The number "9999" is placed in the large-end diameter (LED) column for subsegments containing no logs. The Section and Segment columns will be added between the Transect and Subsegment fields by SnagPRO upon successful importation. The Qualify column is filled by SnagPRO once a formula has been selected. Three additional fields to the right are also reserved for the Tally 2, Tally 3, and Tally 4 columns.

Stratum	Location	Transect	Subsegment	LED	Endpoint	Large	Small	Length	Condition	Qualify	Use	(Species)	(%Length)	EstimLength
1	6	1	1	9999										
1	6	1	2	9999										
1	6	1	3	9999										
1	6	1	4	9999										
1	6	1	5	9999										
1	6	1	6	9999										
1	6	1	7	9999										
1	6	1	8	37	1	37	37	0.4	1		0	9		
1	6	2	1	9999										
1	6	2	2	9999										
1	6	2	3	9999										
1	6	2	4	9999										
1	6	2	5	9999										
1	6	2	6	46	0	37	37	1.4	2		5	3		
1	6	2	6	78	0	41	41	4	2		0	3		
1	6	2	7	9999										
1	6	2	8	9999										
1	9	3	1	9999										
1	9	3	2	52	0	41	36.5	5.6	1		0	2		
1	9	3	2	58	1	52.3	35.4	9.6	1		4	2		
1	9	3	3	58		35.4	29.6	3.2	1		0	2		
1	9	3	4	33	0	23.4	17.2	4	1		1	3		
1	9	3	5	9999										
1	9	3	6	38	1	37.5	36.3	1	1		2	2		
1	9	3	6	44	1	44	42	1.2	1		2	2		
1	9	3	6	49	1	48.5	45.1	1.6	1		2	2		
1	9	3	6	44	1	44.1	38.9	2.6	1		1	2		
1	9	3	6	34	1	33.8	20.6	4.8	3		4	2		
1	9	3	7	39	1	38.6	34.8	3.6	2		1	2		
1	9	3	8	9999										

Figure 9—Example of correct formatting and column placement of strip-plot method (SPM) data before importing into SnagPRO. All columns would be filled only if all variables were measured. Each beginning subsegment of a transect is given the number "1." The number "9999" is placed in the large-end diameter (LED) column for subsegments containing no logs. The Section and Segment columns will be added between the Transect and Subsegment fields by SnagPRO upon successful importation. The Qualify column is filled by SnagPRO once a formula has been selected.

LIM—For each log that meets the stipulated criteria and is intersected along a transect, record the following for all variable estimates (fig. 8):

- Stratum number
- Transect number
- Subsegment number
- Large-end diameter (diameter at largest end of log)
- Intersect diameter
- Condition class (weight estimates) or decay class (weight estimates and wildlife studies)
- Tally (count of endpoints within 2 m [or 6 ft] of transect line for log density estimates)

Optional fields are location, species, and length. Location can correspond to (1) the stand number in which the transect originates or (2) the transect starting position determined by the UTM coordinates of the transect starting point, as established with use of a GPS unit. For subsegments containing no logs, enter "9999" in the LED column.

SPM—For each log that meets the stipulated criteria within the strip-plot boundaries along a transect, record the following for all variable estimates (fig. 9):

- Stratum number
- Transect number
- Subsegment number
- Large-end diameter (diameter at largest end of log)
- Endpoint (refer to fig. 4 to determine whether the endpoint of the log lies within the plot boundaries for density estimates)
- Large diameter (diameter at largest part of log within the plot boundaries)
- Small diameter (diameter at smallest part of log within the plot boundaries)
- Length (length of entire or part of qualifying log within the plot boundaries)
- Condition class (for weight estimates) or decay class (for weight and wildlife studies)

If only density estimates are of interest, enter "1" in the Endpoint column for logs whose endpoints fall within the strip plot. Then enter the diameter of the large end of the log in the LED column. Remember that the LED can lie within or outside the plot boundaries. Enter "9999" for subsegments where no endpoints are within the boundaries. Also, if no logs are encountered within a subsegment, indicate this by recording "9999" in the LED column. Figure 4 demonstrates log endpoints inside versus outside strip plots. Figure 5 shows endpoints on different types of logs.

User-defined fields may also be recorded during surveys, but only include this data in columns to the right of those needed in the CSV file (figs. 8 and 9) for importing to SnagPRO. Additional habitat variables may also be included, such as seral stage of the stand, distance to the nearest edge, and the presence of cut logs or stumps that indicate past timber harvest or firewood cutting.

Header row variables may also be recorded for each log: (1) forest, (2) district, (3) subwatershed, (4) observer, (5) date, and (6) pages. Because the data recorded for each of these variables may be redundant, data columns are set to the far right of the data entry spreadsheet. This enables easy viewing of the data while providing a permanent record of each of these variables for future referencing.

As with snag and tree sampling (Bate and others, in press), we recommend sampling 10 transects (4,000 ft or 1000 m) within each stratum for a pilot sample. For a stratum dominated by smaller, more abundant logs, 10 transects may provide the desired precision to meet sampling objectives.

Importantly, strip-plot boundaries should be established with a measuring stick oriented parallel to the ground, rather than perpendicular to observer's body. This is a concern in steep terrain.

SnagPRO Analysis (Step 7)

In this section, we provide the general background, statistics, and discussion of each function and page within SnagPRO. For detailed operating instructions and examples, refer to the "Tutorial" section. For a brief outline of necessary steps to conduct analyses on a single-stratum landscape, see appendix 4. For stratified landscapes, see appendix 5. No two data sets will be the same size, and SnagPRO was designed to accommodate these variations. Data sets will differ by log variable, number and type of strata, and sample size.

Data entry—

To enter and analyze data, follow these steps:

1. Open **LIMdata.xls** or **SPMdata.xls**.
2. Activate the **Data Entry** sheet.
3. Click on **Move or Copy Sheet** under the **Edit** menu.
4. Check the box **Create a copy**.
5. Under **To book** click on **New Book**.
6. Rename the new file, and then use this sheet to make hard copies for fieldwork.

No two data sets will be the same size, and SnagPRO was designed to accommodate these variations. Data sets will differ by log variable, number and type of strata, and sample size.

When using hand-held computers, activate the data sheet and complete the process from step 3. Depending on sampling objectives, not all fields on the data form may be necessary during field work or data entry, and users may choose to hide some columns. All mandatory columns, however, must be present (unhide) in the CSV import file or the SnagPRO import will fail.

To save data as a CSV file:

1. Activate the data entry sheet.
2. Select **Save As** from the **File** menu.
3. Scroll to find CSV (comma delimited) (*.csv).
4. Click **Save**.

Only the active sheet is saved. To keep the original file intact, save the file with a different extension. Figures 8 (LIM) and 9 (SPM) illustrate the correct formatting needed to successfully import to SnagPRO.

Consecutive plots—

We strongly recommend that users scroll through the entire data set before importing it to SnagPRO, ensuring that each transect has a unique ID and eight subsegment lengths, with the first subsegment numbered as "1." Otherwise, the analysis for optimal transect length will join subsegments from different transects.

Importing files—

For the import to SnagPRO, the application prompts users for initial information. For example, the first message box to appear in SnagPRO asks users to indicate what habitat component—logs or snags and trees—will be analyzed. Select **Logs** so that SnagPRO will expect the specific field names and column arrangement from the import file. SnagPRO then opens the **Log Analysis** portion. Selecting **Snags or Trees** will cause the SnagPRO import to fail. See Bate and others (in press) for correct snag and tree data formatting.

Log Analysis opens to a window that says "SnagPRO-Log Analysis with LIM." If data are collected using LIM, the file is ready to be imported. For data collected using SPM, however, users need to:

1. Select **SPM** from the **Method** menu.
2. From the **File** menu, select **Open**.
3. Navigate to where the CSV data file is stored, and select the file by clicking on **Open**.

Correctly formatted files will open promptly to the Single/Combined page in SnagPRO with the message, "Status: Data file read" in the bottom left-hand corner. This page is where the data set is stored while working in SnagPRO.

If SnagPRO fails to import the file, users will see the message, "An invalid column header was found." If users know that they selected the correct file to import, there may be a problem with formatting. Copy the entire data set into a new file, including only the rows and columns with data. Then repeat the process above.

SnagPRO automatically inserts two columns into the data set after a successful import, labeled "Section" and "Segment." SnagPRO combines the subsegments of varying lengths into newly created sections and segments, resulting in four transect lengths: 12.5, 25, 50, and 100 m or 50, 100, 200, and 400 ft.

Default transect lengths—

Different sampling objectives may require different transect lengths. To override SnagPRO's defaults, navigate to **Settings** and select **Transect Lengths**, then place the cursor within each box to enter the correct length(s). Remember that for optimal transect length analyses, transects should be twice as long as sections; sections twice as long as segments; and segments twice as long as subsegments.

Preselected transect lengths—

For analyses using a single transect length, navigate to **Settings** and select **Transect Length**. Turn the checks on to indicate that a particular length will be included in the analysis, or off to disregard that length. If users did not collect data using long transects, but wanted only segment lengths, users must follow the same protocol for SnagPRO analysis. That is, identify each transect with a unique numeric identifier, and then divide into smaller subsegments. During the CSV import, SnagPRO creates and populates the Segment column, so users only need to check it for inclusion in the analysis.

Species—

Three options are available for selecting species of logs:

- All species
- One species, excluding all others
- Exclude a single species

SnagPRO's default values include all species in the analysis, providing a choice to exclude a single species. For analysis of a single species, click on **Single** under the **Species** menu. To return to the default, click on **Multiple** under the **Species** menu.

Formulas—

SnagPRO evaluates each log using four criteria before a formula is placed in the Qualify column:

- Sampling method used (LIM or SPM);
- Measurement system used (metric or English);
- Log variables of interest (density, percent cover, total length, volume, or weight);
- Log information provided by the user.

The first three criteria above are absolute fields. Once chosen by the user, the criteria for the formula placed in the Qualify column are set. The fourth criterion is a relative field and is evaluated using the four criteria below:

- LED
- Length
- Condition (sound or rotten)
- Species

If information was not collected on the length or condition of the log, this is not a problem, enter "0" when the log length input box appears. If species information was not collected, enter "9999."

SnagPRO's formulas are "If, then" statements. If the log meets all the target criteria specified by the user, then ">0" is placed in the qualify column. If the log fails to meet all the target criteria, then a "0" is placed in the column.

SnagPRO evaluates LED and length based on the minimum value users provide. Condition class is based on a maximum value that users want considered. The condition class is necessary for weight estimates and refers to whether the log is sound or rotten (Brown 1974). Decay classes for wildlife use may also be used. Bull and others (1997) suggested that three log structural classes are sufficient to describe the extent of decay in logs. Decay classes 1 and 2 are sound logs. Decay class 3 represents rotten logs.

If users want to calculate the cover of logs in a particular size class (for example, 25 to 50 cm [10 to 20 in] LED), separate CSV files for specific size classes can be established in a spreadsheet or database program and then imported separately into SnagPRO.

Sorting data sets—
SnagPRO automatically sorts data sets into strata so that each stratum can be analyzed individually, while the entire data set remains on the Single/Combined page. This feature is important because few subwatersheds are homogeneous enough to forgo stratification. Optimal plot size across strata is likely to differ because of differences in log characteristics. Click the **Apply and Sort** button on the **Stratum 1** page to have SnagPRO sort data and place it on the appropriate page.

SnagPRO's equations—

Equations used in SnagPRO assume a normal distribution (Krebs 1989), yet logs are rarely normally distributed across a landscape. Logs typically occur in clumps. Therefore, a minimum of 60 samples is usually needed to ensure that assumptions of normality are met. Consult with a statistician if users are unsure as to whether their data meet this assumption. Avoid overlapping of transects because the equations assume sampling without replacement (i.e., that logs are not sampled twice).

There are two ways to calculate density with LIM. The first uses the reciprocal of the length of each log. This method is inefficient and imprecise compared to SPM (Bate and others 2004). If density estimates are based on log lengths, however, select the **Density** variable under the **Formula** menu. Density estimates from LIM data using metric measurements are obtained using a variation of equation 11 of De Vries (1973). His equation uses log lengths in decimeters; whereas the equation we use measures log lengths in meters:

$$\text{Logs per hectare} = \left(\frac{5\pi 10^3}{L_m}\right)\sum_{}^{n}\left(\frac{1}{l_{m_i}}\right) \qquad [1a]$$

where

L_m = length of transect (meters),

n = number of logs intersected, and

l_{m_i} = length (meters) of the ith log intersected.

Density estimates from LIM data expressed in English units are calculated by using equation 11 of De Vries (1973):

$$\text{Logs per acre} = \left(\frac{21780\pi}{L_{ft}}\right)\sum_{}^{n}\left(\frac{1}{l_{ft_i}}\right) \qquad [1b]$$

where

L_{ft} = length of transect (feet),

n = number of logs intersected, and

l_{ft_i} = length (feet) of the ith log intersected.

The second method for obtaining density estimates with LIM is a simple tally of log endpoints within 2 m or 6 ft of the transect line. This is the same approach as SPM, where density estimates are calculated by summing the number of logs whose endpoints (LEDs) fall within the 50 m² (600 ft²) strip plots, and converting to the number of logs per hectare or acre. This calculation is called **Tally** (found under the **Formula** menu) because it is meant to be used in conjunction with LIM. We recommend this approach if all log variables are of interest and log abundance is high (table 2). In this situation, field observers simply tally the number of qualifying logs whose endpoints fall within 2 m or 6 ft of the transect line (fig. 4), while recording intersect diameters for all other variables. This precludes the need to measure log lengths. One limitation to this approach is that the LED data need to be categorical. If continuous data are required, use a separate SPM field form for density estimates. If more than four size classes are of interest, it is probably more efficient to also use a separate SPM field form for density estimates. Density estimates from the **Tally** method are obtained by using the same approach as for SPM density estimates. For SPM estimates, choose **Density** from the **Formula** menu.

For estimates of total log length, users select the variable **Length** from the **Formula** menu. Metric estimates of total log length using LIM are obtained by using equation 12 of De Vries (1973), which counts the number of logs intersected:

$$\text{Total length of logs (m) per hectare} = \frac{n\pi 10^4}{2L_m} \qquad [2a]$$

For estimates of total length using English measurement units, the following equation is used (DeVries 1973):

$$\text{Total length of logs (ft) per acre} = \left(\frac{21780 n\pi}{L_{ft}} \right) \qquad [2b]$$

Estimates of total log length with SPM are obtained by summing the total length (m or ft) of all portions of qualifying logs that fall within the 50 m² (600 ft²) strip plots, and then converting to total log length per hectare. For logs that traverse subsegment boundaries, log length is the length of log within each individual subsegment (fig. 10).

Mean and median log lengths can be calculated with LIM or SPM; both approaches yield valid estimates of mean log length (Bate and others 2004). With LIM, entire log lengths must be measured. When the **Length** variable is selected under the **Formula** menu, users will see a button labeled **Calculate Mean Length**. Clicking on this button provides the mean and median log lengths. Estimates of both parameters are of interest because they vary with stand history. In unharvested stands, mean and median log lengths will be about equal. In harvested stands, however, the median log length tends to be a fraction of the mean log length.

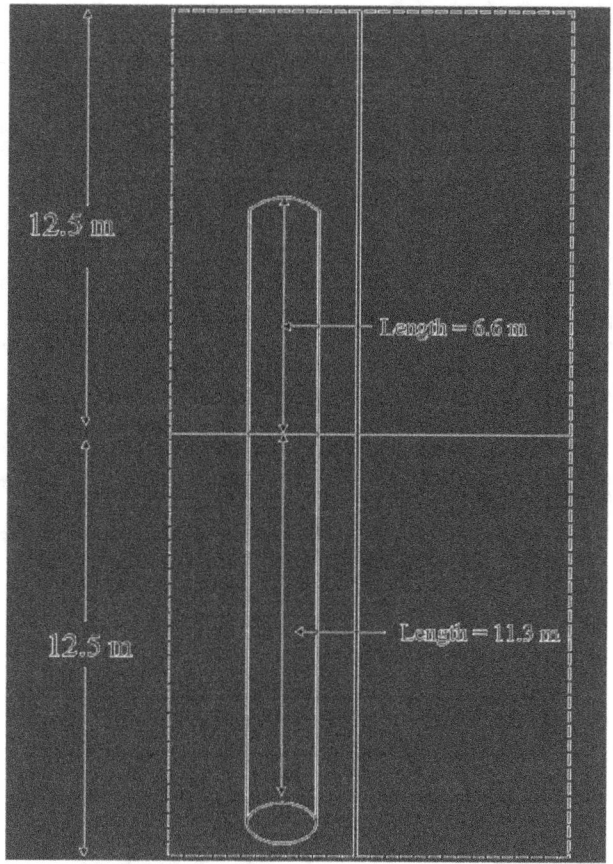

Figure 10—For a log whose bole extends into two subsegments (two 12.5-m transects), the length should be measured separately in each strip plot.

To obtain estimates of mean log length with SPM, users must measure the length of each qualifying log within the strip plot, and also estimate what percentage of the log is contained within the plot in increments of 10 (10 to 100 percent). This is referred to as "% Length" on the field form. If this column is filled on the imported CSV file, SnagPRO will automatically calculate the estimated log length and place the value in the EstimLength column.

Users select the variable **Percent Cover** from the **Formula** menu to obtain estimates of log cover. Estimates of cover with LIM can be obtained using a modification of equation 7 of De Vries (1973). This equation, expressed in metric units, incorporates the diameter (cm) at the point of intersection:

$$\text{Percent Cover} = \left(\frac{\pi}{2L_m}\right)\left(\sum_{i}^{n} d_{cm_i}\right)$$ [3a]

where

d_{cm_i} = diameter (cm) of log i at point of intersection.

Estimates of log cover with LIM in English units is based on the same modified equation 7 of De Vries (1973) incorporating the diameter in inches at the point of intersection:

$$\text{Percent Cover} = \left(\frac{4.1603\pi}{L_{ft}}\right)\sum_{}^{n} d_{in_i} \qquad\qquad [3b]$$

where

d_{in_i} = diameter (in) of log i at point of intersection.

Estimates of log cover with SPM are obtained by measuring the small and large diameters of all qualifying logs, or portions of logs, within the boundaries of the strip plot. The average of the two diameters is then multiplied by the length of each log within the boundaries, to obtain the area (m² or ft²) of each trapezoid-shaped area or log. This value is then converted to the percentage of each strip plot covered by logs.

Volume estimates when using SnagPRO can be obtained by selecting the **Volume** variable under the **Formula** menu. For volume estimates, the intersect diameter needs to be squared. This is the value that is placed in the Qualify column when running volume calculations with LIM. These values are used in the following equation for metric measurements (De Vries 1973; equation 8):

$$\text{Volume (m}^3\text{/ha)} = \left(\frac{\pi^2}{8L_m}\right)\sum_{}^{n} d_{cm_i}^2 \qquad\qquad [4a]$$

For English measurements, the intersect diameter in inches is placed in the Qualify column:

$$\text{Volume (ft}^3\text{/ac)} = \left(\frac{37.8125\pi^2}{L_{ft}}\right)\sum_{}^{n} d_{in_i}^2 \qquad\qquad [4b]$$

To obtain estimates of volume using SPM, each log, or portion of a log, is treated as a cylinder. This requires measurements of the length, and large and small diameters of each portion of log contained within the strip plots (table 1). The volume of all cylinders, or logs, within each strip plot is then converted to either cubic meters per hectare or cubic feet per acre depending on the measurement system in use.

For estimates of weight, the final log variable, select the variable **Weight** from the **Formula** menu. Along with the condition (sound or rotten), weight estimates also rely on the diameter at intersection (De Vries 1973, equation 9) when using LIM. These values are then placed in the Qualify column before calculating weight estimates. For metric measurements using LIM, the following equation is used:

$$\text{Weight (metric tons/ha)} = \left(\frac{\pi^2 S}{8L_m} \right) \sum_{i}^{n} d^2_{cm_i} \qquad [5a]$$

where

$S =$ specific gravity of each log relative to density of water (0.4 is the constant used for sound wood, whereas 0.3 is used as the constant for rotten wood).

We used 400.5 and 304.36 kg/m³ for metric measures of specific gravities for sound and rotten wood, respectively. These are the weights of a solid relative to water density (1000 kg/m³). For English specific gravities, we used 24.96 and 18.72 lb/ft³ for sound and rotten wood relative to the density of water (62.4 lbs/ft³) (Brown and See 1981, DeVries 1973).

For English measurements of weight we used the following equation (DeVries 1973, equation 9):

$$\text{Weight (tons/ac)} = \left(\frac{1.17975\pi^2 S}{L_{ft}} \right) \sum_{i}^{n} d^2_{ft_i} \qquad [5b]$$

Estimates of log weight when using SPM are obtained by multiplying the volume of each log by its specific gravity based on the wood condition.

Analysis by transect length—

Nonstratified stand or landscape—Values in the Qualify column must be summed and subtotaled for each of the four transect lengths. Once SnagPRO has been opened, data imported, and the Qualify column is filled, sum the qualifying log values for a nonstratified stand or landscape with these steps:

1. Click on the **Summarize Statistics** tab.
2. Click on the **Single/Combined** circle in the "Analyze Data From" section.
3. Click **Calculate Statistics**.

SnagPRO calculates subtotals, displaying the average, standard deviation (Std. Dev.), and current number of samples (N) for each transect-length increment on the Summarize Statistics page. These calculated averages, standard deviations, and current number of samples are copied to the Optimal page as well.

Stratified landscapes—Once data have been sorted and the Qualify column is filled, sum the qualifying log values for a stratified stand or landscape with these steps:

1.   Click on the **Summarize Statistics** tab.
2.   Click on the **Stratum 1** circle in the "Analyze Data From" section.
3.   Click **Calculate Statistics**.

Repeat this process for each additional stratum. Results are displayed on the Summarize Statistics and Optimal pages.

Averages are calculated by using the equation:

$$\bar{x} = \frac{\sum x_i}{n} \qquad\qquad [6]$$

where

$\bar{x}$ = sample mean,

x_i = value of x observed in sample i, and

n = total number of samples.

Standard deviations are obtained by the equation:

$$s = \sqrt{\frac{n\sum x_i^2 - \left(\sum x_i\right)^2}{n(n-1)}} \qquad\qquad [7]$$

where

s = sample standard deviation.

Optimal transect length—

On the Optimal page, the statistics for each subsegment, segment, section, and transect across the landscape, or within a unique stratum, are displayed on individual pages as indicated by each tab. For data taken from a nonstratified landscape or stand, click on the tab labeled **Single/Combined**. Note that for each stratum, the Optimal plot size analysis needs to be run separately. The Qualifying Logs box, immediately above the Stratum tabs, allows for a text description of the current query, which is useful when working with different size classes and conditions.

The box labeled Precision Level Desired is set at the default of 0.2. This default setting calculates how many samples are required to be within 20 percent of the true mean. If, however, users find that the sample sizes required to obtain this level of precision is cost-prohibitive, this box may be changed to something broader, such as 0.25. The box labeled t-value also is set at a default of 1.67. This is the Student's t-value for a 90-percent confidence interval if 60 samples have been taken. This also may be changed to meet user objectives.

Under the column headings Average and StDev, find the estimated average and standard deviation, respectively, for the summed values for each of the four transect-section lengths. In the next two columns to the right, users will find the parameter estimate and its variance, respectively, expressed in terms of units per hectare or acre. The variance is calculated by the following equation:

$$s^2 = \frac{\sum(x_i - \bar{x})^2}{n-1}$$ [8]

The next two columns, Estimated Sample Size Required (n) and Estimated Total Survey Distance Required, calculate the total number of transect sections and total length of transect, respectively, required to obtain a parameter estimate that is within 20 percent of the true mean 90 percent of the time. The required sample size is determined by (Cochran 1977):

$$n = \left(\frac{t_\alpha s}{d}\right)^2$$ [9]

where

Generally, whichever requires the shortest transect length is considered optimal, because it allows users to obtain the most precise estimate with the smallest amount of effort.

n = sample size required to estimate the mean,

s = standard deviation of the mean within each plot size,

t_α = Student's t-value for a 90-percent confidence interval ($\alpha = 0.10$), and

d = desired absolute error (default value is set at 20 percent of the pilot mean).

To select the optimal transect length within a stratum, look at the column labeled Estimated Total Survey Distance Required. Which transect section requires the shortest length of transect? Generally, whichever requires the shortest transect length is considered optimal, because it allows users to obtain the most precise estimate with the smallest amount of effort. Use this transect section length for subsequent analyses to obtain a parameter estimate with a bound.

To the right, users will see a column labeled Minimum Transect Required. This is set at 1000 m or 3,281 ft and represents the minimum transect length that we recommend be sampled before any conclusions are drawn. (See the "Confidence Intervals for Parameters" section for details.) The next column, labeled Current Number of Samples Collected (N), shows how many samples have been collected in each of the four transect length categories. The column labeled Additional Samples

Required calculates how many additional meters or feet of transect are required given that some samples have already been taken. The final column on the Optimal page provides users with the parameter estimate in English units if the data are in metric, and in metric units if the data are English.

Analysis for independence—
The sampling protocols presented here suggest sampling along 100-m or 400-ft-long transects divided into smaller increments so that the optimal transect length may be determined. Sampling units were assumed to be independent (Hurlbert 1984, Krebs 1989, Swihart and Slade 1985) for equations in this report; therefore the length of transect chosen as optimal should also be tested to ensure that the density (or cover, length, volume, or weight) of logs on one increment of a transect are not predicted by the density of logs in the previous increment. If they are, sampling units would be serially correlated, and this would violate the assumption of independence.

SnagPRO tests for a serial correlation between increments of similar length along transects. Users will find this function on the Summarize Statistics page. Follow these steps:

1. Fill in the Qualify column with the appropriate formula.
2. Click **Calculate Statistics** for the stratum of interest.
3. Click **Correlation** on the Summarize Statistics page.
4. Enter the name of the transect length increment to test for serial correlation.

Results of the test provide a Pearson's correlation coefficient and the coefficient of determination. The correlation coefficient (r) estimates the association between two variables (Sokal and Rohlf 1981). The coefficient of determination (r^2) is the correlation coefficient squared. It estimates the dependence of one variable upon another. Using density as an example, the r^2 value explains how much the density in one increment is predicted by the previous increment.

The range for correlation coefficients is $-1 < r < +1$ (Sokal and Rohlf 1981). High correlation coefficients suggest that adjacent length increments along the same transect (for example, subsegments, segments, or sections) are correlated with each other and cannot be considered independent sampling units. As a general guideline, correlation coefficients less than 0.45 ($r^2 < 0.2$) suggest that adjacent increments are independent and the increment selected can be used as the sampling unit. Values higher than this suggest adjacent increments are correlated and sampling should continue, with the optimal transect length indicated through initial analyses of pilot data or by choosing a different transect length that appears to be independent.

For example, if segments are shown to be the optimal transect length within a stratum, but these segments are serially correlated with each other, there are two choices. First, drop the suggested sampling protocol along 100-m or 400-ft transects, and continue sampling only with segment lengths. In this situation, continue with the standardized numbering of transects and subsegments, but only sample a segment length (25 m or 100 ft) along each transect. Second, test for independence of subsegment or section lengths. If either of these lengths are independent, use one of these lengths (nested within the 100-m-long transect) for sampling.

Parameter Estimates for a Nonstratified Landscape—
To obtain estimates of a variable and its precision for a nonstratified stand or landscape, users should click the tab with the variable name they are calculating (**Density**, **Percent Cover**, **Total Length**, **Volume**, or **Weight**) and then on the **Simple-Random Sampling Equation** tab.

Clicking on the **Single** button activates the simple-random sampling equations. Users of SPM will be prompted to enter the size of their stand or landscape (hectares or acres) in the **Landscape Area** box before filling in the page. The size of the stand or landscape is necessary for area plot sampling so that a finite population correction factor (Krebs 1989) can be applied in cases where the area sampled represents a large proportion of the entire landscape.

When the **Single** button is clicked, SnagPRO automatically fills in the needed cells from the Optimal page using information from the transect length increment that minimized sampling effort. The variable estimate, its standard error, bound, upper and lower limits, and the current level of precision are all given below.

Users may also override the optimal transect length and choose the transect length they want to evaluate. This would be done if, for example, results from subsegments were serially correlated, but segments were not. In this example users would:

1. From the **Settings** menu, select **Optimal Selection**.
2. Click on **Single** stratum.
3. Select **Segments**.
4. Click on the **Single** button on the variable page again.

To change back, just choose **Auto** from the selection menu and re-click the **Single** button.

> **Users may also override the optimal transect length and choose the transect length they want to evaluate. This would be done if, for example, results from subsegments were serially correlated, but segments were not.**

Parameter estimates for a stratified landscape—

To obtain estimates for a stratified stand or landscape, click the tab with the name of the desired variable. Activate the **Stratified Random Sampling Equation** page by clicking on the tab with this name. For LIM analyses, click on the tab labeled **Stratified** to have information transferred to this sheet. For SPM analyses, enter the area of each stratum before clicking the **Stratified** button. Then SnagPRO automatically fills in the necessary cells from the Optimal page using information from the transect length that minimized sampling effort for each stratum. The variable estimate, its standard error, bound, upper and lower limits, and the current level of precision are all provided.

As with a single stratum, users may also override the optimal transect length for each stratum following the directions above. This may occur when transects are chosen as the optimal length within a certain stratum, but results in a substantial length of transect required within that stratum. If more sampling is required, examine sample size requirements for various transect lengths before deciding on a length.

Sample size determination—

The estimated sample size for nonstratified landscapes or stands is given on the Optimal page under Estimated Sample Size Required (n) and is converted to meters or feet in the next column.

For stratified subwatersheds, go to the **Sample Size** page. SnagPRO provides both the proportional allocation and optimal method for sample size estimates, breaking it down into transect lengths for each stratum.

Proportional Allocation of the sample size allocates the samples among the strata based on the proportion of the total area in each stratum (weight W_i). By contrast, **Optimal Allocation** incorporates both the stratum proportional area (W_i) and variance (s^2_i) to determine how many samples are required within each stratum (Krebs 1989). Both methods calculate the number of samples required to obtain a parameter estimate that is within 20 percent of the true mean 90 percent of the time.

The sample size (Krebs 1989) required by the proportional allocation method is determined by the equation:

$$n = \frac{t_\alpha^2 \sum W_i s_i^2}{B^2}$$ [10]

where

n = total sample size required in stratified sampling,

B = desired bound for $1 - \alpha$, we have substituted the symbol B (to denote bound) for the d listed in Krebs (1989) equations,

t_α = student's t value for 90-percent confidence limits ($1 - \alpha$),

W_i = stratum weight (A_i/A),

s_i^2 = variance in stratum i,

A = total number of hectares in landscape, and

A_i = number of hectares in stratum i.

The number of samples within each stratum (n_i) is determined by multiplying the total number of samples needed (n) by the weight (W_i) of each stratum.

$$n_i = nW_i$$ [11]

Sample size for the optimal allocation method (Krebs 1989) is found by the following equation:

$$n = \frac{\left(\sum W_i s_i\right)^2}{\left(\frac{B}{t_a}\right)^2 + \left(\frac{1}{A}\right)\left(\sum W_i s_i^2\right)}$$ [12]

where

s_i = standard deviation in stratum i.

The number of samples needed within each stratum is estimated by:

$$n_i = n\left(\frac{A_i s_i}{\sum A_i s_i}\right)$$ [13]

Each of the allocation methods has its advantages and disadvantages. The proportional allocation method offers the advantage of dropping the stratification and combining all samples after the sampling is done, such as when users find little or no difference in parameter estimates across strata. This yields a larger sample size (n) and a smaller variance. This option is not available if the optimal allocation method is used.

The optimal allocation method, however, provides the best estimate for the least cost in situations where large differences in a variable exist across strata. With this method, sampling is concentrated in the stratum that has the highest variance. By contrast, proportional allocation concentrates sampling effort in the largest stratum, regardless of the variance within each stratum.

It is important to remember that the sample sizes given are only estimates of the number required to obtain a desired precision. Consequently, we recommend that data be analyzed periodically to gauge the precision of estimates.

Confidence intervals for parameters—
A minimum of 60 samples for the landscape, or 20 samples from each stratum (whichever is higher), are required before the mean density (or other variables) of logs can be estimated. Analysis can then be done to evaluate whether enough samples have been collected to achieve objectives. See the "Establishing Transects" section of this report for an exception to the minimum number of samples required.

The two analysis options for evaluating adequacy of sample size are (1) estimate average parameter and (2) compare to target parameter. Both allow the user to either obtain an average log parameter that is within 20 percent of the true mean at a desired confidence level, or determine whether the estimated value is significantly different from the targeted value, respectively. Users may choose both options. Go to the **Densities (Percent Cover, Total Length, Volume,** or **Weight)** page to obtain an estimated average for the parameter of interest.

Estimate average parameter—
This option requires one of two equations based on which sampling method— simple or stratified random—is used. To see these equations, go to the **Densities (Percent Cover, Total Length, Volume,** or **Weight)** page.

For the simple random sampling method, the average is calculated in the standard way (equation 6). The variance is calculated by:

$$s_{\bar{x}} = \sqrt{\frac{s^2}{n}} \qquad\qquad [14]$$

where

$\bar{x}$ = population mean,
n = sample size,
s^2 = variance of the measurements,
$s_{\bar{x}}$ = standard error of the mean $\bar{x}$, and

The confidence interval is calculated using a normal approximation (Krebs 1989):

$$\bar{x} \pm t_\alpha s_{\bar{x}} \qquad [15]$$

where

t_α = Student's t value for 90-percent confidence limits (1 - α).

As in the previous sheets, all shaded boxes require input from the user. The t-value is preset at 1.67, for a sample size equal to 60 to obtain a 90-percent confidence interval. If a different level of confidence is desired, the t-value can be changed. In the first section of each variable sheet, an estimated mean is given based on simple random sampling methods.

In the second section, a parameter estimate with a bound is calculated based on stratified random sampling methods. The stratified mean for each variable is computed by the following equation:

$$\bar{x}_{st} = \frac{\sum_{i=1}^{L} A_i \bar{x}_i}{A} \qquad [16]$$

where

$\bar{x}_{st}$ = stratified population mean (number per hectare),
$\bar{x}_i$ = observed mean in stratum i,
A_i = number of hectares in stratum i,
A = total number of hectares in subwatershed,
i = stratum number, and
L = number of strata.

To calculate a confidence interval, the stratified variance must first be determined:

$$\text{Variance of} \quad (\bar{x}_{st}) = \sum_{i=1}^{L} \left(\frac{W_i^2 s_i^2}{n_i} \right) \qquad [17]$$

where

n_i = number of samples in stratum i,
s_i^2 = variance in stratum i, and
W_i = stratum weight or proportion of area in stratum i (A_i/A).

Then the confidence interval is calculated by the normal approximation:

$$\overline{x}_{st} \pm t_\alpha \left(\sqrt{\mathrm{var}(\overline{x}_{st})} \right) \qquad [18]$$

SnagPRO is designed to accommodate landscapes with different numbers of strata; therefore, the user must enter the correct number when prompted by the **Number of Strata** message box. This tells SnagPRO which equation to use. We set the limit at four strata because it is rare that more than four sampling categories will be used. In particular, with increasing number of strata comes the law of diminishing returns. That is, for each additional stratum, there needs to be an additional 10 transects (100 m or 400 ft) of sampling line. If, however, resource specialists find that they need to divide a landscape into five or more strata, they can use the **Simple-Random Sampling Equation** page within SnagPRO to obtain their stratum means (equation 6) and variances (equation 8) and then calculate a stratified mean estimate and its bound using equations 16 through 18.

Compare to Target Density—
The second parameter option is an informal statistical test that allows users to determine whether the estimated log value (density, cover, etc.) is significantly different from the targeted value identified as part of their standards and guidelines. A minimum of 60 samples for the landscape, or 20 samples from each stratum (whichever is higher), are required. For subwatersheds >2800 ha (7,000 ac) it may be necessary to increase sampling effort to compensate for the natural variability of logs owing to elevational gradients and other environmental conditions.

Example: A 8097-ha (20,000-acre) subwatershed that encompasses three distinct forest community types may require about 100 samples to adequately conduct the Compare to Target Density test. This translates into an increase of about 1.5 transects (100 m long) for every 405 ha (1,000 ac) surveyed above 2800 ha (7,000 ac). This option is especially useful in situations where densities are low and the sampling effort is necessarily high to obtain an estimate within 20 percent of the true mean (90 percent of the time). Sampling is designed to assess whether the subwatershed meets management guidelines for logs. See the "Establishing Transects" section for details in transect establishment.

The t-test is the most common way to test for a significant difference between two means. The t-test compares the mean along each transect to the target mean. This works well in single-stratum landscapes, but becomes complicated where different transect lengths or widths are used. Consequently, SnagPRO uses confidence intervals to compare means among multiple samples (Zar 1984).

Confidence intervals can be used to evaluate whether the targeted value is different than the estimated value. The bound on the parameter estimate is calculated by using a t-statistic, so is analogous to a t-test and approximates the same distribution as the Student's t-test statistic. This approach simplified the process with stratified landscapes.

The statistical comparison to estimate whether the targeted value falls within the confidence interval of the estimated value can be used after meeting the minimum number of samples. The **Statistical Test** page in SnagPRO enables users to graph the estimated and targeted densities of a sample to visually display whether they are significantly different. Users simply enter the targeted value and the estimated value and its bounds from the log survey; the resulting graph is automatically plotted. See example 2 in the "Tutorial" section for specific details.

Wildlife Use Signs

Documenting the degree of wildlife use of logs may be of interest. For example, users may want to identify which log species, log diameter, or length class is associated with the most foraging signs by woodpeckers. This can be done with SnagPRO and SPM data. Analysis of wildlife use is only available with SPM data because this method was found to be more accurate than the LIM in predicting wildlife use (Bate and others 2004). Wildlife use that could be visually detected, such as woodpecker foraging or middens, was evaluated by Bate and others (2004).

SnagPRO can evaluate every log for five factors: (1) LED, (2) length, (3) condition, (4) species, and (5) wildlife use. (The main utility of the **Wildlife Use** function is to estimate use by wildlife.) Percentage of logs used by wildlife is calculated by dividing the number of logs with wildlife use by the total number of logs encountered.

$$P_u = \frac{L_s}{L_t} \times 100 \qquad\qquad [19]$$

where

P_u = percent use,

L_s = number of logs with wildlife use signs, and

L_t = total number of logs available or encountered.

Tutorials

Example I: Metric Weight and Density Estimates for a Single Stand With LIM and SPM Tally

Background example—
In the tutorial, we describe a specific example of how our log sampling methods can be used. In our example, managers are interested in assessing log conditions in a 24-ha, mixed-conifer stand before a seed-tree harvest to determine how much downed woody material should be retained during harvest. Specifically, the goal is to estimate the weight and density (within 20 percent of the true mean, with 90 percent confidence) of logs that are ≥1 m long and ≥15 cm LED. The stand is relatively steep with slopes averaging 60 percent. The stand is buffered on most sides by young and mature stands. Weight of logs by species also is of interest, and consequently, log species are recorded.

Stratification—
In our example, a ground check revealed no evident differences in log distributions inside, versus along the edges, of the stand. Consequently, the stand is treated as a single stratum. A combination of sampling methods is selected to meet objectives. For estimates of weight, the LIM is used because log density appears to be moderate (6 to 11 logs per 100 m of transect), but travel will be difficult (table 2). The SPM tally method will be used to estimate density.

Pilot survey—
Because of the steepness of the slope, pairs of transects that are perpendicular to each other are established. Five pairs of transects (10 transects) are established by placing a grid over a map of the stand, and then randomly selecting 10 grid points for the starting point of each transect. Starting points are paired together based on their proximity to each other. The first transect of each pair is set in a random compass direction, and the second transect is set 90 degrees from the first direction.

Each 100-m transect is then divided into eight 12.5-m-long subsegments. Each transect is assigned a unique numeric identifier while numbering the subsegments 1 through 8. This is done so that during the computer analysis of field data, the shorter subsegments can be joined into 25- and 50-m-long transect sections to determine the optimal transect length. For transects extending beyond stand boundaries, the "bounce-back" method is used to keep the transect within the sampling area while continuing to sample with standardized transect lengths to include stand edges (fig. 7).

Field forms are secured by making copies of the data entry sheet found in the file named **LIMdata.xls** (fig. 8). (See "Field Forms" under "General Surveying Procedures" for complete details.) Field copies of appendix 2 are made to describe the sample information required under each field heading.

In the field, all intersected logs based on a minimum specific size (≥1 m long and ≥15 cm LED) are sampled. For each log intersected, the following information is collected for weight estimates:

- Species
- Diameter (cm) at intersection
- Diameter (cm) of LED for size class analyses
- Condition (sound = 1; rotten = 2) (Brown 1974)

A log did not have to be intersected by the transect line to qualify for the SPM tally.

For subsegments where no logs are intersected, "9999" is entered in the LED column.

For density estimates, logs were tallied if they met minimum size requirements and had endpoints (fig. 4) within 2 m of the transect line. This number was entered in the column labeled "Tally 1." For subsegments containing no log endpoints, a "0" was placed in the Tally 1 column (fig. 8). Recall that a log did not have to be intersected by the transect line to qualify for the SPM tally (fig. 4).

Data entry—

Use Sheet 1 of the file **LIMdata.xls** to enter data. In our example, data have been entered as part of the process described above. Open the file **LIMdata.xls** and click on the tab in the lower left corner, labeled "Tutorial Data-I." Here you will find that the log data collected from 10 transects have been entered for this stand. Also notice that although the Length and Qualify columns are empty, they are still included so that the correct format is maintained (fig. 8).

Consecutive subsegments—

Before analyses, sort transects and subsegments in ascending order to ensure that eight subsegments compose each transect. In Excel, click a single cell in the first row and then click **Data | Sort**. Make sure that the entire data set has been highlighted for sorting. Then select **Sort By** transect and **Then By** subsegment. Scroll through the entire data set to ensure that eight subsegment lengths have been entered for each transect, and the beginning subsegment of each transect is numbered "1."

Creating a CSV file—

SnagPRO imports only CSV files. To create a CSV file, follow these steps:

1. Activate the Tutorial_data_I sheet by clicking anywhere on the sheet:
   Select File | Save As.

2. Click **Save as Type** at the bottom of the Save As message box.

3. Select "CSV (comma delimited)(*.csv)."

4. Assign a new file name in the File Name box.

5. Click **Save**. When saving as a CSV file, only the active sheet is retained. By saving the file with a different name, the original file is kept intact.

6. Click **OK** and **Yes** for first and second warning boxes, respectively.

Importing to SnagPRO—

Import the CSV file of log data using these steps:

1. Launch SnagPRO by double-clicking on the desktop icon or the executable file— SnagPRO.exe.

2. Click **Logs**.

3. Go to **Measurement** and click **Metric**.

4. Go to **Method** and click **LIM**.

5. Go to **File | Open**. In the message box, Look In, browse to the folder containing the CSV data and select the file name.

This process should successfully import the CSV file. Note that additional columns have been added to your file. First, the Section and Segment columns were inserted between Transect and Subsegment. And second, SnagPRO combined consecutive subsegments (12.5-m lengths) into segments (25-m lengths), and segments into sections (50-m lengths) to allow for optimal transect length analysis.

Formula entry—

The next step is to have SnagPRO fill in the appropriate formula in the Qualify column. This formula determines which logs are included in the current analysis. To do this, click on **Weight** under the **Formula** menu on the Single/Combined page. Then click on **Set Criteria** button located in the bottom-left of the screen.

To create the correct formula, based on sampling objectives, enter:

1. "15" for LED

2. "0" for Length (the default when log lengths are not measured)

3. "9999" for Species (all logs are considered)

SnagPRO evaluates each log according to the criteria listed above. For logs meeting all criteria, SnagPRO takes the intersect diameter of each log, squares it, and then multiplies it by the appropriate specific gravity, 0.4 and 0.3 for sound and rotten logs, respectively. The values contained in the Qualify column are then used in the LIM estimator (equation 5a) to obtain weight estimates.

Analyzing by transect length—

SnagPRO now calculates averages and standard deviations for each transect length within each stratum on the Summary Statistics page. To calculate the statistics for the current forest conditions:

1. Click on the **Summary Statistics** tab.
2. Click on the **Single/Combined** circle in the "Analyze Data From" section.
3. Click on the **Calculate Statistics** button.

SnagPRO subtotals the values for each transect length (Subsegment_12.5, Segment_25, Section_50, and Transect_100) (fig. 11). The number on the end of each label gives the length of transect in meters. To the right of the subtotaled values are

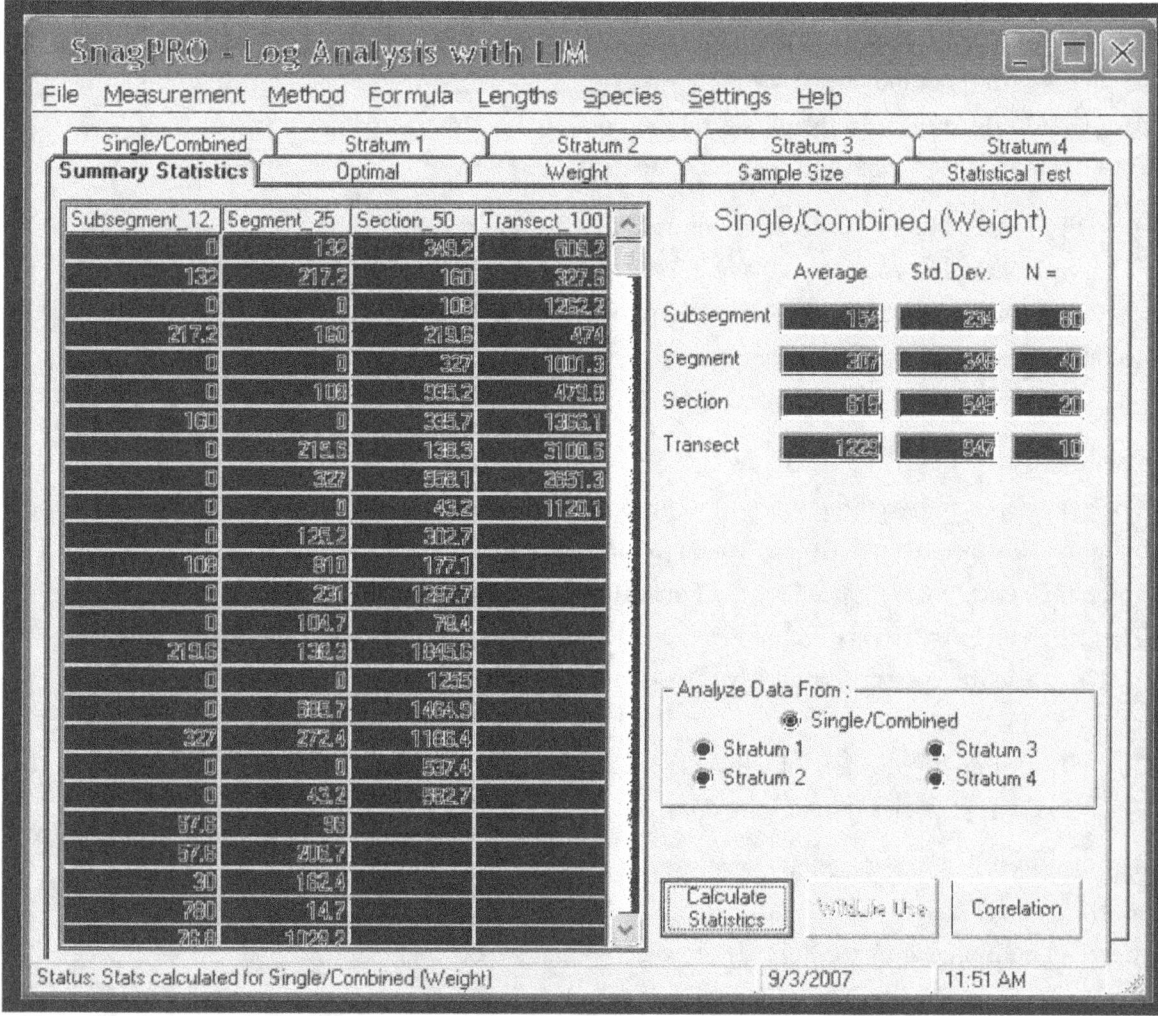

Figure 11—**Summary Statistics** page: averages, standard deviations, and number of samples to the right of summed values for each transect length for analysis using LIM to obtain log weight estimates. Data are from the Tutorial Data-I sheet in the LIMdata.xls file.

the averages, standard deviations, and current sample sizes for each transect length. These values were simultaneously transferred to the Optimal page (fig. 12).

Optimal transect length—

To determine the transect length that optimizes sampling, switch to the **Optimal** page (fig. 12). First, write a brief description of the study area and log characteristics included in this sample in the box labeled **Qualifying Logs**. For example, for this analysis you might write:

Qualifying Logs: Stand 709; logs ≥15 cm LED; ≥1 m long.

Under the heading **Single/Combined** on the Optimal page, each transect is listed by name and length. The column Average provides the estimated average

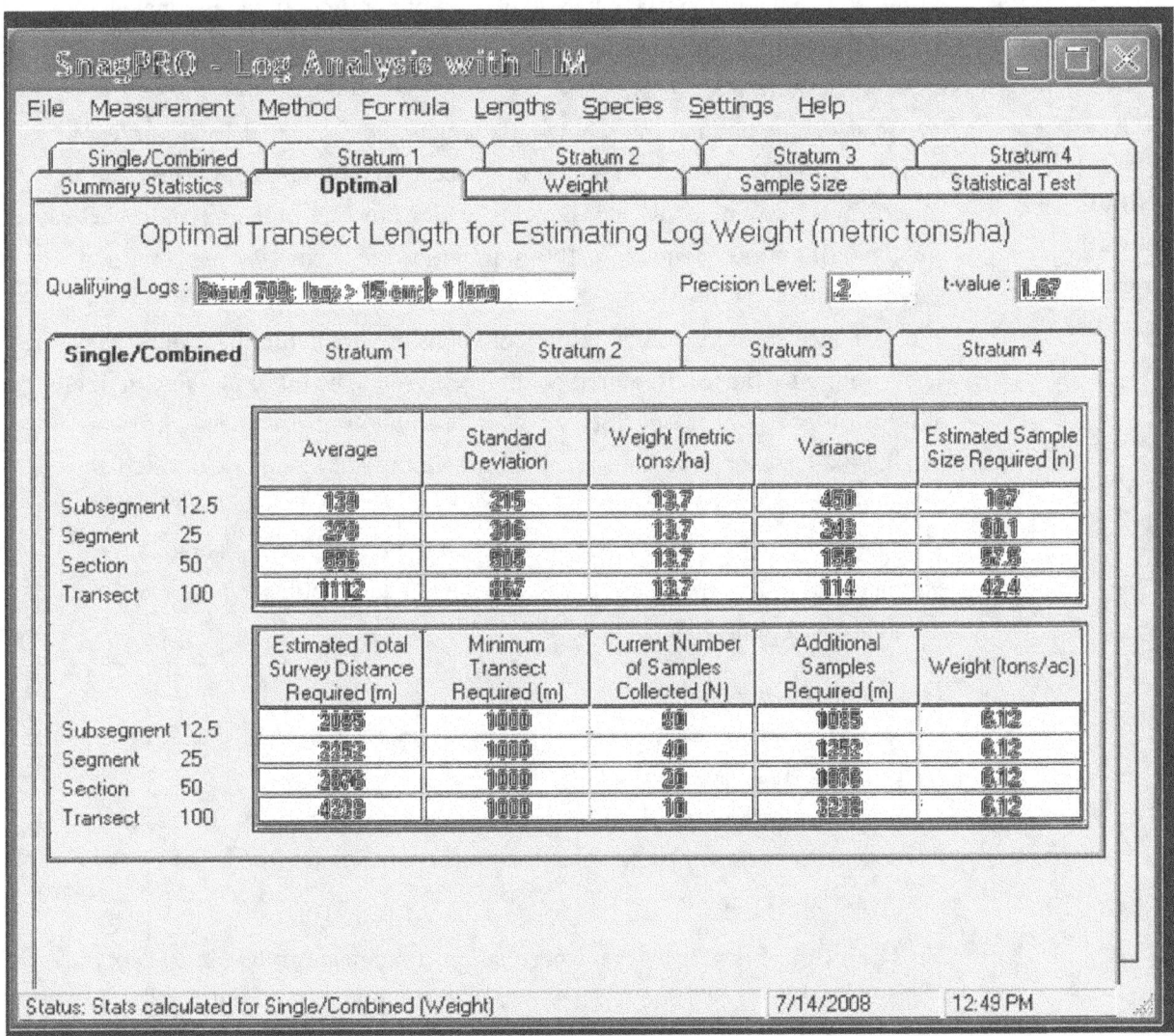

Figure 12. **Optimal** page: optimal transect length analysis for obtaining weight estimates of logs in single stand. Results show estimated log weight and estimated transect length required using each of four transect lengths. Data from the Tutorial Data-I sheet in the LIMdata.xls file.

values (squared intersects multiplied by specific gravity) from the Qualify column for the four transect lengths. Standard deviations for these same values are shown in the next column.

Under Weight (metric tons per hectare), the averages from the Qualify column have been converted to actual weight measurements (fig. 12) using equation 5a. Similarly, the standard deviations for each length are inserted into the equation to obtain an estimate of the variance. For our example, SnagPRO estimates that the stand supports about 15.2 metric tons/ha of logs in this size class. Notice that the English equivalent is given in the last column of this section (about 6.8 tons/ac). The column Estimated Sample Size Required calculates the total number of sampling units (expressed in transect sections) required to obtain a weight estimate that is within 20 percent of the true mean 90 percent of the time. In the Estimated Total Survey Distance Required column, the sampling units required are expressed in total length of transect.

To select the optimal transect length, look at the Estimated Total Survey Distance Required column. Which transect section requires the shortest transect length?

To select the optimal transect length, look at the Estimated Total Survey Distance Required column. Which transect section requires the shortest transect length? In this example, the subsegments, which are 12.5-m long, require the least amount (2012 m). By contrast, if 100-m transects are used, 4140 m of transect length would be required.

We stated earlier that SnagPRO's equations require a minimum of 60 samples. The Minimum Transect Required column represents the minimum length in meters of transect for a pilot sample. See the "Establishing Transects" section for more detail. SnagPRO then evaluates the Current Number of Samples Collected and calculates the Additional Samples Required. For this example, a little over 1000 m of additional sampling (about 10 transects) would be required to obtain a weight estimate within 20 percent of the true mean with a 90-percent confidence interval. But are subsegments independent?

Test for independence—

To test for independence, switch to the **Summary Statistics** page and run the serial correlation test. To do this:

1. Click on the **Correlation** button in the bottom-right corner of the screen.
2. Enter "Subsegment" when the first message box appears labeled Correlation Length.

The message box displays the correlation coefficient ($r = 0.083$) and coefficient of determination ($r^2 = 0.0069$). The low r^2 value (0.0069) implies that adjacent subsegments along a transect are independent sampling units. Consequently, subsegments can be used for the remainder of the analysis along 100-m transects. One caveat here: remember to rerun this analysis when sampling is completed to ensure independence of sampling units.

Weight analysis—

Assuming all sampling has been completed, the final weight estimate, its bound, and precision level are given on the **Weight** page (fig. 13). To obtain these values, follow these steps:

1. Click on the **Weight** tab.
2. Click on the **Simple-Random Sampling Equation** tab.
3. Click the **Single** button under the **Calculate** heading.

Our example results indicate that the stand supports an estimated 15.2 ± 4.31 metric tons/ha of logs ≥15 cm LED and ≥1 m in length (fig. 13). The precision of

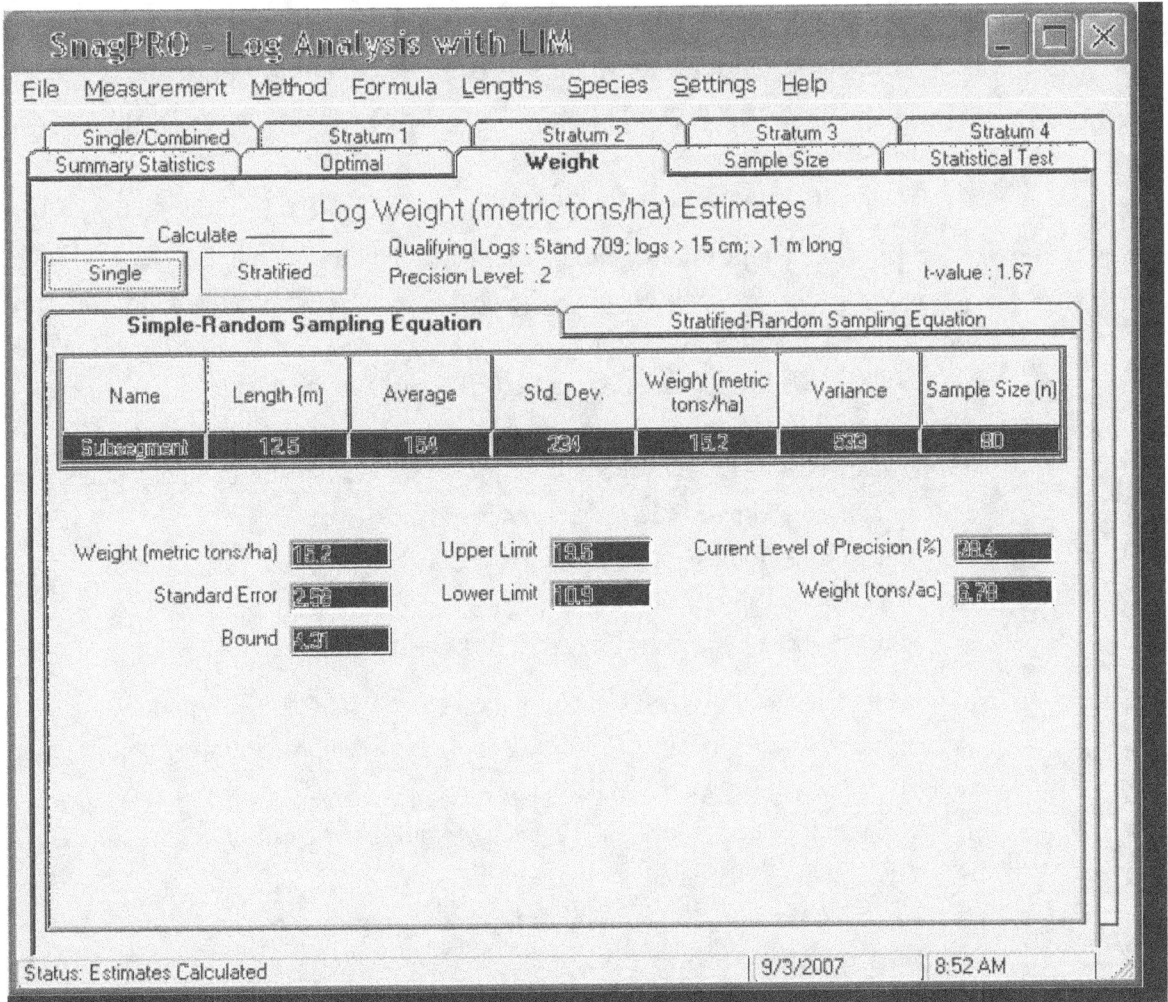

Figure 13—**Weight** page: estimated log weight, standard error, bound, upper and lower limits, and current level of precision for estimates in a single stand. Data are from the Tutorial Data-I sheet in the LIMdata xls file.

an estimate is calculated by dividing the bound by the mean. In this example, the bound of 4.31 is divided by the mean of 15.2, and then multiplied by 100. The result is 28.4 percent, which states that you are 90-percent confident that your density estimate is within 28.4 percent of the true mean.

Density analysis by tally—

The next step is to obtain density estimates using the tally data. To do this:

1. Click on **Tally** from the **Formula** menu. (Notice that the **Formula** list also includes **Density**, but this calculation is performed only if log lengths have been measured.)

2. Click **Yes** when asked "Do you want to clear this analysis and reload the current database?"

3. Click the **Set Criteria** button.

4. Enter "Tally 1" when asked for the name of the column you would like to tally.

5. Click on the tab at the top of the screen labeled **Summary Statistics**.

6. Click on the **Single/Combined** circle under the section labeled "Analyze Data From."

7. Complete the process by clicking on the **Calculate Statistics** button.

Switch to the **Optimal** page to determine which transect length is best for density estimates. Example results estimate that the stands contain 248 logs/ha (100 logs/ac). Looking under the Estimated Total Survey Distance Required column, we see that subsegments again appear to be the optimal transect length within this stand. They require only 1242 m of transect. Therefore, only two or three more transects are needed to reach the desired precision. But are subsegments independent for density estimates? To test for independence:

1. Switch back to the **Summary Statistics** page.

2. Click on the **Correlation** button.

3. Enter "Subsegment" into **Correlation Length** box.

The message box displays the correlation coefficient ($r = 0.115$) and the coefficient of determination ($r^2 = 0.013$) for log densities. Similar to the weight correlation analysis, subsegments appear to be independent.

To obtain the current level of precision of your density estimate:

1. Click on the **Tally** page tab.

2. Highlight the **Simple-Random Sampling Equation** tab.

3. Click the **Single** button.

4. Enter "24" into the **Single Stratum** box.

It is estimated that there are 248 ± 53.8 logs/ha in this stand. Precision is just below 22 percent.

Conclusions for single-stand weight and density analysis—

From the pilot survey data alone, the desired precision for density has nearly been reached. To obtain this precision for weight, however, about 10 additional transects would have to be sampled. If, however, the current precision of 28 percent is deemed adequate, sampling can cease. If it is deemed important to improve precision to ≤20 percent, then the 10 additional transects should be surveyed.

Example II: English Parameter Estimates and Statistical Test for a Stratified Landscape Using SPM

Background information—

A second example is forest compliance monitoring for wildlife, specifically to evaluate whether log management goals have been met on a landscape scale. The landscape comprises mixed-conifer forest communities. Many areas have been clearcut or seed-tree harvested. The remaining stands are mature or old-growth forests.

Current wildlife guidelines stipulate retention of an average of 20 logs/ac and >2 percent log cover across the landscape (composed of logs with a LED >10 in and >6 ft long). The monitoring goal is to estimate both density and percentage cover within 20 percent of the true mean 90 percent of the time to evaluate guidelines. Woodpecker and small mammal use of logs also is of interest within the different forest structural conditions.

Stratification—

Aerial photographs show that the landscape is highly fragmented and geospatial data verify that clearcut and seed-tree harvests have been the primary methods of timber harvesting. Therefore, stands will be placed into one of two strata: (1) harvested or (2) unharvested mature/old-growth stands. A map of the stand polygons for each stratum is established with GIS. Each stand's acreage and the total acreage within each stratum is summed. There are 750 and 224 ac in strata 1 and 2, respectively. Field reconnaissance is then done to verify that each stand has been placed in the proper stratum.

Pilot survey—

An initial reconnaissance indicates that it is uncommon to intersect >10 large logs (>10 in LED and >6 ft long) per 330 ft of transect (see table 2 for details). Furthermore, sampling must be as efficient as possible because of substantial travel required to sample at random points across the landscape. Consequently, SPM is selected as the sampling method. Also, LED data are collected as a continuous variable so that analysis can be done on a variety of size classes.

Five stands in each stratum are randomly selected in which two 400-ft-long transects are established (fig. 6). Starting points for each transect are selected by randomly placing a grid over each stand and randomly choosing a grid intersection for the starting point. The compass direction is also random.

Each transect is assigned a number, and then divided into eight 50-ft subsegments, numbering them 1 through 8 so that during analysis, the shorter subsegments can be joined into 100-ft (segments) and 200-ft (sections) transect lengths. Then SnagPRO can help determine the best transect length for each stratum. The bounce-back method is used for transects heading outside stand boundaries (fig. 7). Continue to sample with standardized transect lengths and include stand edges.

The SPM Field Form sheet found in the file named **SPMdata.xls** (fig. 9) is used as the field form. (See "Field Forms" under "General Surveying Procedures" for complete details.) Appendix 3 is customized to describe the information required under each field heading, as an aid to field sampling, and copies of figures 4 and 5 also are made to help guide fieldwork.

Only the portions of logs >10 in LED and >6 ft long within sampling boundaries are measured. The LEDs of each log are measured as shown in fig. 5. For each log, record:

1. Diameter (in) of large end regardless if it is in or out of the plot.
2. Whether the endpoint of the log (fig. 5) is in (enter 1) or out (enter 0) of the plot.
3. Diameter (in) of largest portion of the log contained within the plot.
4. Diameter (in) of smallest portion of the log contained within the plot.
5. Length (ft) of portion of log contained within the plot.
6. Condition based on three-class decay system (Bull and others 1997).
7. Species.
8. Wildlife use: 0 = no use, 1 = woodpecker foraging, 2 = small mammal middens.

For subsegments where no qualifying logs are encountered, enter "9999" in the LED column.

Data entry—

To enter your own data, use Sheet 1 of the file SPMdata.xls. In our example, data have been entered in Excel as part of the tutorial. Open the file **SPMdata.xls** and click on the tab in the lower left corner that is labeled "Tutorial Data-II." Here you will find that the log data collected from 20 transects have been entered for our example.

Consecutive subsegments—

Before analysis, sort transects and subsegments in ascending order to ensure that there are eight subsegments for each transect. In Excel, click a single cell in the first row and then click **Data | Sort**. Make sure that the entire data set has been highlighted for sorting. Then select **Sort By** transect and **Then By** subsegment. Scroll through the entire data set to ensure that eight subsegment lengths have been entered for each transect and the beginning subsegment of each transect is numbered "1."

Creating a CSV file—

SnagPRO imports only CSV files. To create a CSV file, follow these steps:

1. Activate the Tutorial_Data_II sheet by clicking anywhere on the sheet.
2. Select **File | Save As**.
3. Click **Save as Type** at the bottom of the Save As message box.
4. Select "CSV (comma delimited)(*.csv)".
5. Assign a new file name in the file name box.
6. Click **Save**. When saving as a CSV file, only the active sheet is retained. By saving the file with a different name, the original file is kept intact.
7. Click **OK** and **Yes** for first and second warning boxes, respectively.

Importing to SnagPRO—

Import the CSV file of log data using these steps:

1. Launch SnagPRO by double-clicking on the desktop icon or the executable file—SnagPRO.exe.
2. Click **Logs**.
3. Go to **Measurement**, and click **English**.
4. Go to **Method** and click **SPM**.
5. Go to **File | Open**. In the message box "Look In," browse to the folder containing the CSV data and select the file name.

This should successfully import the CSV file onto the Single/Combined page of SnagPRO. Note that the Section and Segment columns have been added to your file. SnagPRO combined consecutive subsegments (50-ft lengths) into segments (100-ft lengths), and segments into sections (200-ft lengths) to allow for optimal transect length analysis.

Formula entry—

The next step is to have SnagPRO insert the appropriate formula into the Qualify column for each stratum. This formula determines which logs are included in the analysis. To do this:

1. Click on the **Stratum 1** tab to activate the sheet.
2. Click on **Density** under the **Formula** menu.
3. Click the **Apply and Sort** button.

To create the correct formula for all logs >10 in LED, enter

1. "10" for LED.
2. "0" for EstimLength because all logs will be included.
3. "3" for Condition (all decay classes are included).
4. "9999" for Species (all log species included).

SnagPRO evaluates each log for the criteria listed above. For logs meeting all criteria, and with endpoints contained within the plot, SnagPRO places a "1" in the Qualify column. Note that log lengths are based on the EstimLength column rather than the Length column. The Length column only represents the length of the logs within the strip plots and not their entire lengths. EstimLength is the total length of log, both inside and outside the plot. See EstimLength in the "SnagPRO's Equations" section for more information.

Analyzing by transect length—

SnagPRO now calculates averages and standard deviations for each transect length within each stratum on the Summary Statistics page. To calculate the statistics for stratum 1:

1. Click on the **Summary Statistics** tab.
2. Click on the **Stratum 1** circle in the Analyze Data From section.
3. Click on the **Calculate Statistics** button.

To determine the transect length that optimizes sampling in stratum 1, switch to the **Stratum 1** sheet on the **Optimal** page. First, write a brief description of the study area and log characteristics included in this sample in the box labeled "Qualifying Logs." For example, for this analysis you might write:

Qualifying Logs: Stratum 1; >10 cm LED; >1 m long.

To the far left on this page, each transect is listed by name and length. The Average column provides the estimated average values (summed endpoints) from the Qualify column for the four transect lengths. Standard deviations for these same values are shown in the next column. Under Density (logs/ac), the summed endpoints from the Qualify column have been converted to density.

SnagPRO estimates that there are 14.5 logs/ac. Notice that the metric equivalent is given in the last column (35.9 logs/ha). The column Estimated Sample Size Required calculates the total number of sampling units (expressed in number of strip plots) required to obtain a density estimate within 20 percent of the true mean 90 percent of the time. In the Estimated Total Survey Distance Required column, the sampling units required are expressed in total length of transect.

To select the optimal transect length, look at the Estimated Total Survey Distance Required column. Which transect section requires the shortest transect length? In this stratum, the segments, which are 100 ft long, require the least amount (21,905 ft). Notice that the 200-ft lengths (section) are the second-best choice, with 22,226 ft of transect required.

Earlier, we stated that SnagPRO's equations require a minimum of 60 samples. The Minimum Transect Required column represents the minimum length in feet of transect for a pilot sample. See the "Establishing Transects" section for more detail. SnagPRO then evaluates the Current Number of Samples Collected and calculates the Additional Samples Required.

For this stratum, about five times as many segments as have been sampled are needed to obtain a density estimate with desired precision. Sampling effort is high because of low log density and high variance within this stratum. In addition, SnagPRO currently considers this a single landscape, which is necessary to determine the optimal transect length. Sampling effort will be less within this stratum, however, once it is considered in conjunction with stratum 2.

Now check and see if segments can be considered independent sampling units. To do this:

1. Switch back to the **Summarize Statistics** page.
2. Click on the **Correlation** button.
3. Enter "Segment" into the **Correlation** box.

The message box displays the correlation coefficient ($r = 0.105$) and the coefficient of determination ($r^2 = 0.011$) for log densities in stratum 1. Based on these results, adjacent segments can be considered independent and used as the sampling unit for stratum 1.

To determine the optimal transect length for stratum 2, repeat all steps described for stratum 1. The stratum 2 sheet on the **Optimal** page shows that the estimated log density for stratum 2 (mature/old-growth stands) is 39.9 logs/ac and transect lengths (400-ft lengths) appear to optimize the sampling effort (7,754 total ft of transect required).

Stratified density analysis—

To obtain an estimate of the required sample size for the entire landscape, we first need an estimate of the stratified mean density to enter in the sample size equation. To do this:

1. Go to the **Densities** page (fig. 14).
2. Click on the **Stratified Random Sampling Equation** tab.
3. Enter "750" into the Stratum 1 box in the Stratum Size (acres) section.
4. Enter "224" into the Stratum 2 box.
5. Click the **Stratified** button under Calculate.

Once the Stratum Sizes (acres) have been filled in, SnagPRO transfers all statistics from the Optimal page to the Density page. The results on the Density page (fig. 14), estimate an average density of 20.3 ± 5.81 logs/ac. Precision is 28.6 percent.

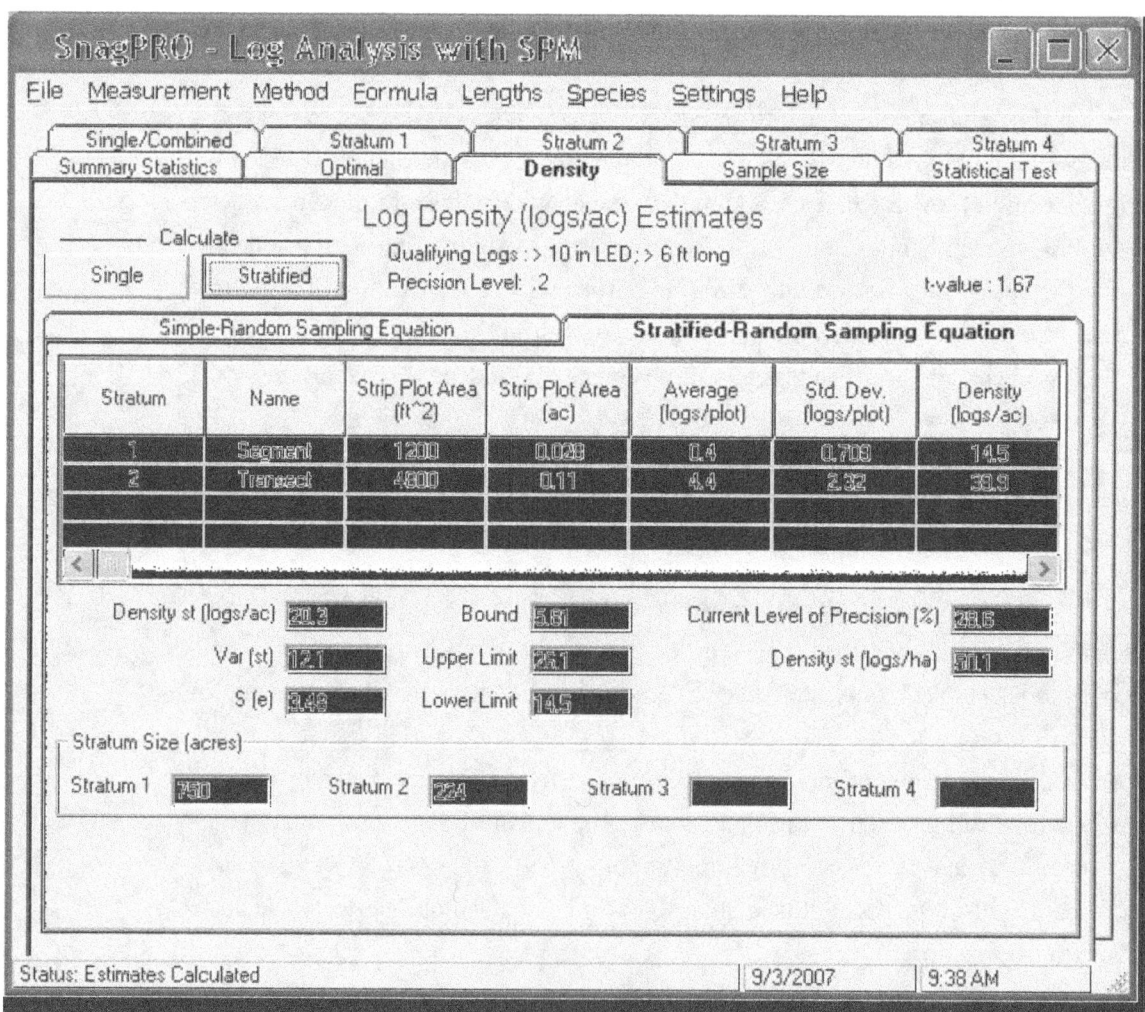

Figure 14—**Densities** page: estimated log density, standard error, bound, upper and lower limits, and current level of precision for estimates in on a stratified landscape. Data are from the Tutorial Data-II sheet in the SPMdata.xls file.

Sample size determination—

The next step is to determine the required sample size to obtain the desired precision. Sample sizes for stratified subwatersheds are calculated on the Sample Size page, so activate this page (fig. 15). Notice that SnagPRO transferred the statistics to the Sample Size page once the stratified density estimate on the Density page was calculated.

At the bottom of the Sample Size page (fig. 15), output from two sample size equations are shown—Optimal Allocation and Proportional Allocation. The optimal allocation method, which incorporates the stratum variance in its

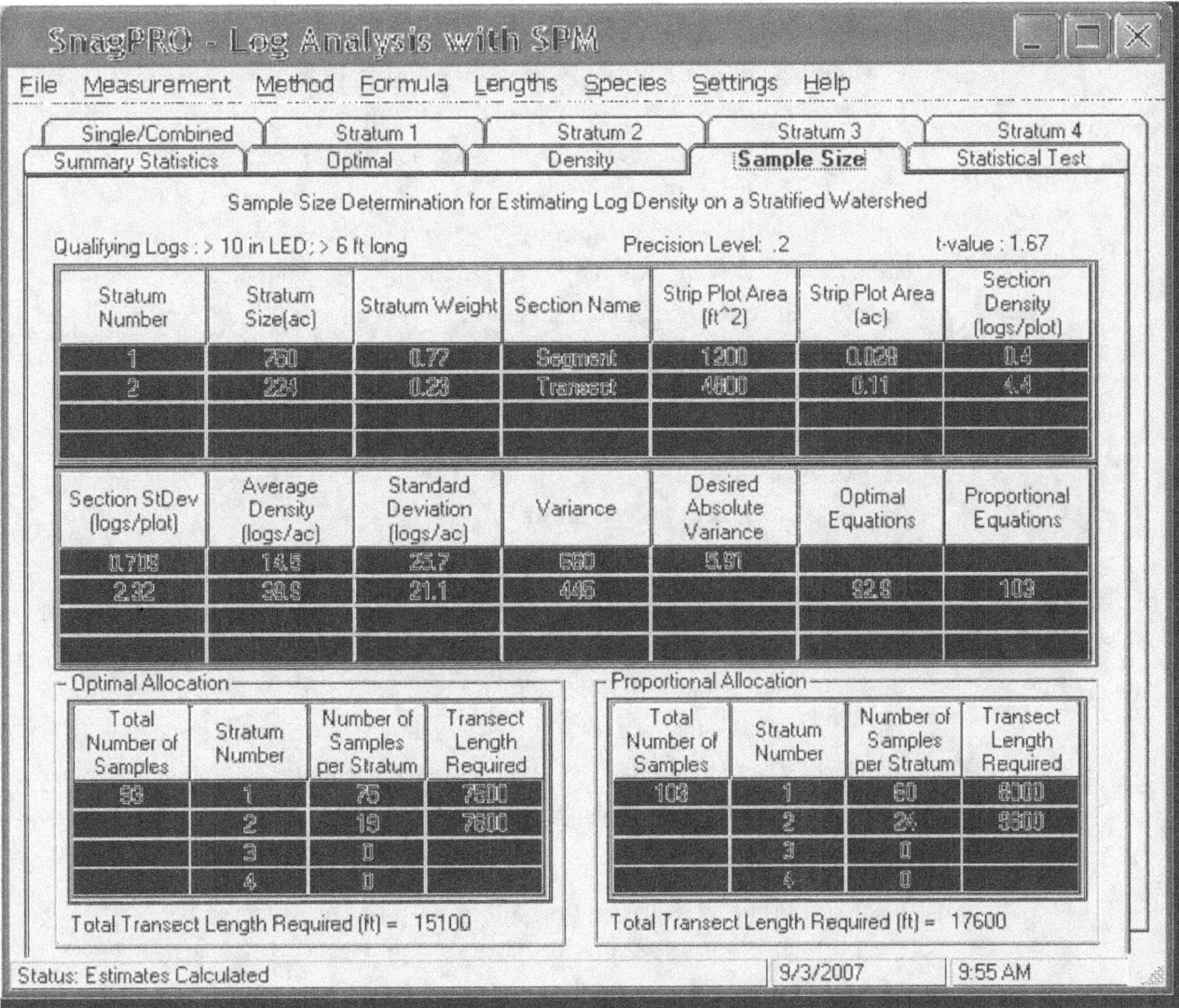

Figure 15—**Sample size** page. Optimal and proportional sample size calculations for obtaining estimates of log density on a landscape containing two strata. Data are from the Tutorial Data-II sheet in the SPMdata.xls file.

> **Both sample size equations agree that additional samples are needed. It is important to remember that sample size requirements may change with additional sampling, owing to changes in the variance of estimates.**

calculations, estimates that 93 samples are required to obtain a stratified mean within 20 percent of the true mean, 90 percent of the time. These 93 samples are then divided between the two strata: 75 samples in stratum 1 (harvested stands) and 19 samples in stratum 2 (mature/old-growth stands). Segments are the sampling unit for stratum 1 and transects are the sampling unit for stratum 2. These estimates are equal to about 7,500 ft of transect in stratum 1 and 7,600 ft in stratum 2. Recall, however, that 4,000 ft of transect have already been sampled in both strata.

On the bottom right of the page is the heading "Proportional Allocation." This method uses the overall variance of the subwatershed and then allocates the samples based on the size of each stratum. Results show that 103 samples are needed to obtain the desired precision, which in turn requires 8,000 ft of transect in stratum 1 and 9,600 ft in stratum 2.

Both sample size equations agree that additional samples are needed. It is important to remember that sample size requirements may change with additional sampling, owing to changes in the variance of estimates. This possibility increases if the pilot sample is ultimately shown to be a poor representation of the variation within a stratum. Consequently, the best way to avoid oversampling (where large sample sizes are required) is to periodically enter your data, and re-run the SnagPRO analysis. In addition, sometimes it is helpful to "override" the default for transect length. For example, what would happen if you changed the transect length to something shorter in stratum 2, such as segments? To do this, follow these steps:

1. From the **Settings** menu, highlight **Optimal Selection**.
2. Click on **Stratum 2**.
3. Check **Segment** instead of Auto.

By overriding the default transect length for stratum 2, precision changes slightly, from 28.6 to 29.2 percent. Sample size requirements, however, drop from 7,600 ft to only 4,800 ft under the optimal allocation method. However, sample requirements in stratum 1 increase to 8,700 ft. These changes demonstrate the sensitivity of the equations and the chosen sample size. Given the uncertainty, it may be best to sample about five additional stands within each stratum, and then reanalyze the data to see how the additional information affects the chosen transect length and precision.

Compare to target density—
Once 60 samples have been collected, the test of whether the estimated density of qualifying logs meets the targeted density of 20 logs/ac can be done. The null hypothesis is that no difference exists between the estimated and targeted log densities.

Go to **Statistical Test** page to conduct the test (fig. 16).

Follow these steps:

1. Enter the targeted density of "20" into the box labeled Target Value.
2. Enter the estimated log density of "20.3 logs/ac" into the box labeled Estimated Value.
3. Enter "5.81" into the estimated Bound box.

Results are automatically plotted as a graph (fig. 16), which shows that the line representing the target density is within the upper and lower limits of the estimated density, just below the targeted density. Consequently, the null hypothesis is not rejected. That is, results indicate, with 90 percent confidence, that the log density on this landscape is adequate to meet agency guidelines.

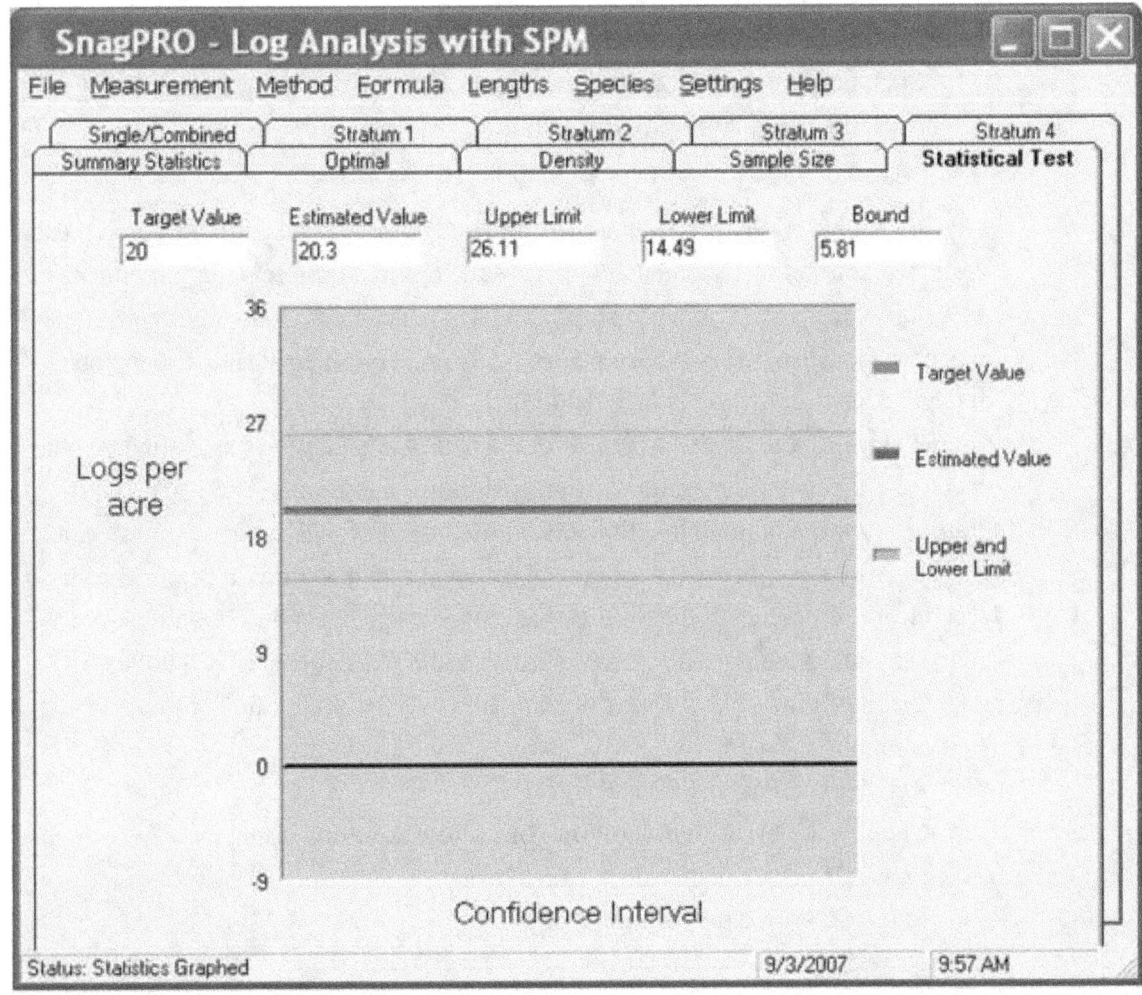

Figure 16—**Statistical test** page. Graph depicting test for significant differences between estimated and targeted densities of qualifying logs on stratified landscape. Estimated value and its bound are from the **Densities** page (fig. 14). Data are from the Tutorial Data-II sheet in the SPMdata xls file.

Percentage cover analysis—

To analyze percentage cover estimates, change the variable selection:

1. Click on **Percent Cover** under the **Formula** menu.
2. Click **Yes** when asked "Do you want to clear this analysis and reload the current data set?"

At this point, the steps to conduct the analysis for percentage cover are identical to the steps taken for the density analysis:

1. Activate the **Stratum 1** page.
2. Click the **Set Criteria** button.
3. Enter the correct log characteristics for LED, EstimLength, Condition and Species.
4. Switch to the **Summary Statistics** page.
5. Click on the **Stratum 1** circle.
6. Click the **Calculate Statistics** button.
7. Click on the **Stratum 2** circle.
8. Click the **Calculate Statistics** button.
9. Switch to the **Optimal** page to view results for stratum 1.

Percentage cover for stratum 1 is estimated to be 0.54 percent. Based on these results, it appears that segment lengths are the optimal transect length requiring 11,872 ft of transect. The serial correlation test conducted on the Summary Statistics page (see instructions above from density analysis) indicates that segments are independent sampling units ($r^2 = 0.0008$).

Clicking on the **Stratum 2** sheet of the Optimal page shows an estimated cover value of 2.6 percent for stratum 2. In this stratum, the subsegments, or shortest transects, are the optimal length. Only 3,666 ft of total transect is required (which has already been collected) to obtain an estimate that is within 20 percent of the true mean, 90 percent of the time. Serial correlation test conducted on the Summary Statistic page also shows subsegments to be independent ($r^2 = 0.0008$).

To conduct the statistical test to compare cover estimates, first obtain a stratified estimate for cover:

1. Activate the **Percent Cover** page.
2. Click on the **Stratified-Random Sampling Equation** sheet.
3. Enter "750" into the Stratum 1 area box.
4. Enter "224" into the Stratum 2 box.
5. Click the **Stratified** button.

Results indicate a stratified estimate of percentage cover of 1.02 ± 0.184. The current precision (18 percent) exceeds the goal of being within 20 percent of the true mean. To test for a difference between targeted and estimated percentage cover, switch to the **Statistical Test** page.

Of interest is whether the estimated cover of logs across this landscape equals or exceeds the targeted value of 2 percent. In this case, the null hypothesis is that no difference exists between estimated cover of logs across this landscape and the target of 2 percent. To test, enter the percentage cover estimate, its bound, and the target value into the appropriate boxes on the Statistical Test page (fig. 17).

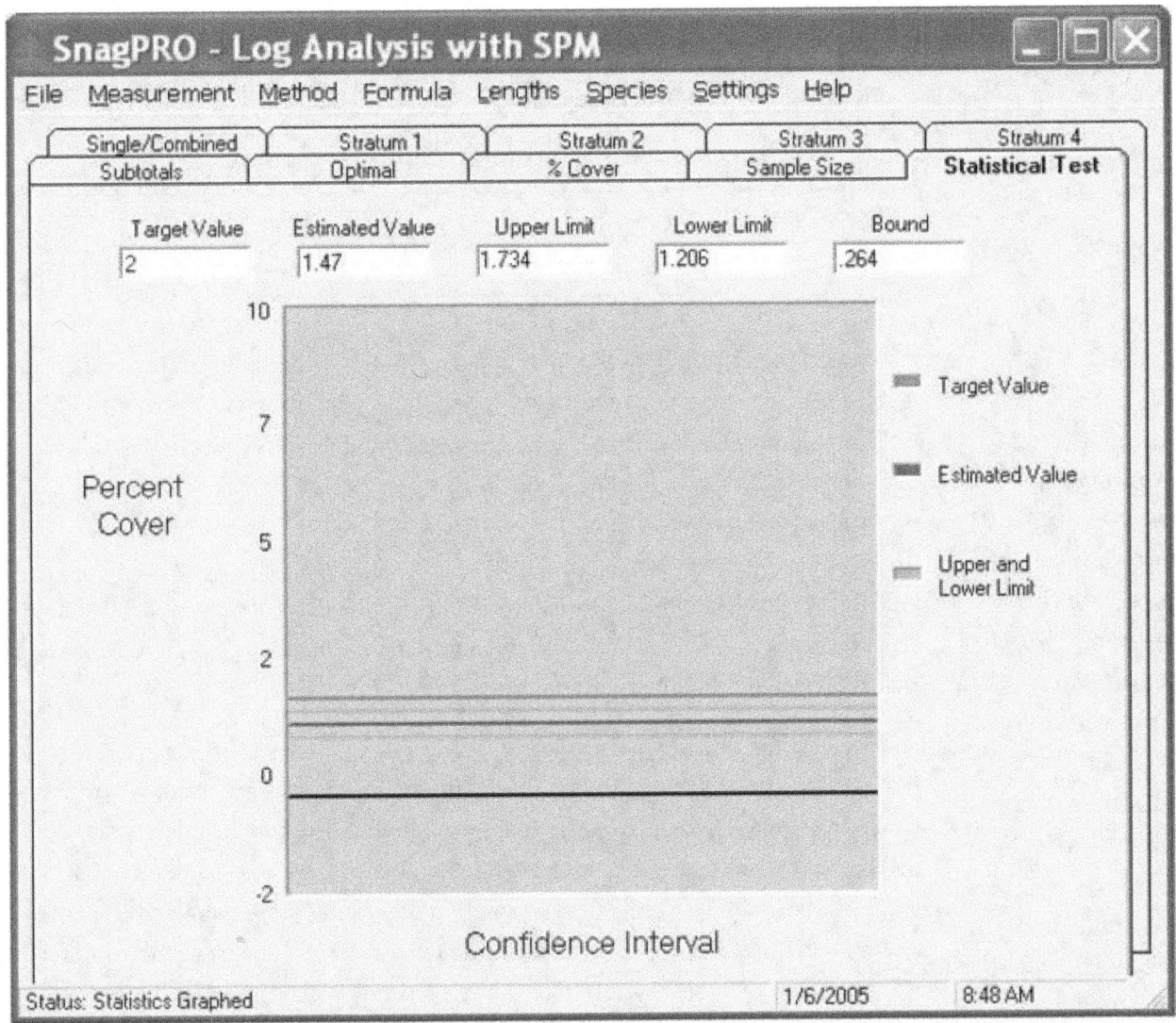

Figure 17—**Statistical test** page. Graph depicting test for significant differences between estimated and targeted percent cover values of qualifying logs on stratified landscape. Estimated value and its bound are from the **Percent Cover** page. Data are from the Tutorial Data-II sheet in the SPMdata xls file.

The resulting graph shows that the red line (top line), representing the target cover, is not within the upper and lower limits of cover estimated for the entire landscape (fig. 17). This is in contrast to the results observed from the density analysis. Therefore, the null hypothesis of "no difference between the harvested and unharvested density estimates," is rejected. Results suggest that you can be 90-percent confident that log cover across the landscape does not equal or exceed the target of 2 percent.

Wildlife use—

The final objective is to evaluate wildlife use of logs in harvested stands versus unharvested stands. To calculate use of logs with signs of woodpecker foraging:

1. Activate the **Summary Statistics** page.
2. Click on the **Stratum 1** circle from the Analyze Data From section.
3. Click on the **Wildlife Use** button.
4. Enter "10" into the message box labeled LED.
5. Enter "0" into the EstimLength box.
6. Enter "3" into the Condition box.
7. Enter "9999" into the Species box.
8. Enter "1" into the Wildlife use box.

Results in the Wildlife section of this page show that within Stratum 1, there were 38 logs available for woodpecker foraging use and 6 showed signs of use for a use of 15.8 percent in harvested stands. For stratum 2, results show that out of 126 logs available, 21 showed woodpecker foraging signs for a use of 16.7 percent in unharvested stands.

For small mammal use (wildlife code = 2) in stratum 1, 38 logs were available and 3 had evidence of middens, resulting in use of 7.9 percent in harvested stands. This compares to 40 out of 126 available logs having small mammal middens, for a use of 31.7 percent in unharvested stands.

Conclusions for multiple strata using SPM—

Statistical tests comparing log estimates with management goals revealed different results. Although log densities met agency guidelines, the percentage of cover did not. These results suggest that an adequate number of logs were retained in harvested stands, but were short in length or small in diameter. Consequently, the small size or short length of logs contributed little toward cover. Results of the wildlife use analysis suggest that woodpecker foraging use was about equal in harvested and unharvested stands. By contrast, squirrel use of logs in unharvested stands was about four times that in harvested stands.

These results suggest that an adequate number of logs were retained in harvested stands, but were short in length or small in diameter. Consequently, the small size or short length of logs contributed little toward cover.

Example III: Metric Parameter Estimates for a Stratified Landscape Using a Combination of LIM and SPM

Background information—

In this example, two resource disciplines are interested in information on log conditions in a subwatershed. Fire managers are interested in volume of logs ≥15 cm LED and ≥1 m long for separate areas within the subwatershed. Wildlife managers need a stratified estimate of log volume for the entire subwatershed, but only for larger logs (≥25 cm LED and ≥1 m long). Both fire and wildlife managers want estimates to be as precise as possible because of pending management actions, but budget constraints may limit the number of stands that can be sampled.

Aerial photographs and geospatial data indicate that less than half the subwatershed has been harvested in the past 40 years. Log volumes are anticipated to be low in these stands. About one-third of the subwatershed is composed of mature forests with pockets of old-growth interspersed. Of special concern, however, are a number of stands that have undergone high mortality owing to an outbreak of spruce budworm (*Choristoneura occidentalis* Free.) (Sheehan 1996) during the past 10 years. Travel is difficult within these stands because of the high log abundance.

Stratification—

Based on a ground reconnaissance, the harvested stands appear to be accurately represented in the GIS database and support a low number of logs. Log density is initially checked by estimating how many logs are intersected by several randomly established transect lines within the typical harvested stand on this subwatershed (see table 2 for details). On average, it appears that three to four logs are intersected with every 100 m of transect in the harvested stands.

The remaining unharvested stands have greater log abundance, and individual stands require visual examination to determine whether abundance is moderate or high. Reconnaissance indicates high log abundance in stands that are undergoing the budworm outbreak; in these stands, over 30 logs per 100-m transect were intersected. The remaining stands appear to support moderate abundance, with an average of 10 to 15 logs per 100 m of transect. Based on this information, three strata are established: (1) recent clearcut and seed-tree harvest units with low log abundance, (2) mature stands with moderate log abundance, and (3) mature stands with high log abundance. For this example there are 812, 654, and 490 ha in strata 1, 2, and 3, respectively.

In strata 2 and 3 where log abundance is moderate and high, respectively, LIM (table 2) is used to sample logs. Because of the low abundance of logs in harvested stands, however, SPM is used for estimates of log volume in stratum 1 to minimize the number of transects required.

Pilot survey—

Five stands from each stratum are randomly selected for sampling. Starting points for each transect are selected by placing a grid over each stand and randomly choosing a grid intersection for the starting point. The compass direction also is randomly determined.

Each 100-m transect is divided into eight 12.5-m-long subsegments. Each transect is assigned a unique numeric identifier while numbering the subsegments 1 through 8. This is done so that the shorter subsegments can be evaluated as 25- and 50-m transect sections to determine the optimal transect length during analysis. The bounce-back method is used to keep the transect within the sampling area that otherwise would extend beyond stand boundaries, while continuing to sample with standardized transect lengths to include stand edges (fig. 7).

The SPM Field Form sheet, found in the file named **SPMdata.xls** (fig. 9), is used as the field form in stratum 1. (See "Field Forms" under "General Surveying Procedures" for complete details.) Appendix 3 is customized to describe the information required under each field heading as an aid to field sampling, and copies of figures 4 and 5 also are made to help guide fieldcrews to determine the appropriate place to measure LED.

Only the portions of logs ≥ 15 cm LED and ≥ 1 m length within the boundaries are measured. The LEDs of each log are measured as shown in figure 5. For each qualifying log, record:

1. Size class (record either 15 for ≥ 15 or 25 for ≥ 25) of LED.
2. Diameter (cm) of largest portion of the log contained within the plot.
3. Diameter (cm) of smallest portion of the log contained within the plot.
4. Length (m) of portion of log contained within the plot.

For subsegments where no qualifying logs are encountered, "9999" is entered in the LED column. For data collection in strata 2 and 3, make copies of the data entry sheet found in the file named **LIMdata.xls** (fig. 8) for use as a field form. (See "Field Forms" under "General Surveying Procedures" for complete details.) Customize appendix 2 to describe the information required under each field heading of the field form, as an aid to fieldwork.

In the field, for each qualifying log intersected, the following volume measurements are recorded:

1. Diameter (cm) at intersection.
2. Size class (either 15 or 25 cm) of LED.

For subsegments where no qualifying logs are intersected, "9999" is entered in the LED column.

Data entry—

When using a combination of LIM and SPM, data from each stratum must be stored separately because of differences in data collection techniques and equations. First, obtain an estimate of the variable of interest (in this case, volume) for each stratum. Then estimates from each stratum can be entered in a special page in SnagPRO named **Combination** found under the **Method** menu. Estimates of the stratified mean, precision level, and sample sizes within each stratum and across the landscape are then calculated on this page.

To enter LIM data analysis, use Sheet 1 of the file **LIMdata.xls**. For SPM analysis, use Sheet 1 of the **SPMdata.xls** file. For this example, however, the data have already been entered. For LIM analysis, open the file **LIMdata.xls** and click on the tab in the lower left corner that is labeled "Tutorial Data-III-Stratum 2." Here you will find log data collected from 10 transects for this stratum.

Consecutive subsegments—

Before analyses, sort transects and subsegments in ascending order to ensure that there are eight subsegments for each transect. In Excel, click a single cell in the first row and then click **Data | Sort**. Make sure that the entire data set has been highlighted for sorting. Then select **Sort By** transect and **Then By** subsegment. Scroll through the entire data set to ensure that eight subsegment lengths have been entered for each transect, and the beginning subsegment of each transect is numbered "1."

Creating a CSV file—

SnagPRO imports only CSV files. To create a CSV file for stratum 2, follow these steps:

1. Activate the "Tutorial_Data_III-Stratum 2" sheet by clicking anywhere on the sheet.
2. Select **File | Save As**.
3. Click **Save as Type** at the bottom of the Save As message box.
4. Select "CSV (comma delimited)(*.csv)."
5. Assign a new file name in the file name box.
6. Click **Save**. When saving as a CSV file, only the active sheet is retained. By saving the file with a different name, the original file is kept intact.
7. Click **OK** and **Yes** for first and second warning boxes, respectively.

To create the CSV file for stratum 3, repeat the procedure above with the worksheet labeled "Tutorial_Data_III-Stratum 3" found in the **LIMdata.xls** file. To create the CSV file for stratum 1, repeat the procedure above using the worksheet labeled "Tutorial Data-III" found in the **SPMdata.xls** file.

Importing to SnagPRO—

Import the CSV file of stratum 2 log data using these steps:

1. Launch SnagPRO by double-clicking on the desktop icon or the executable file—SnagPRO.exe.
2. Click **Logs**.
3. Go to **Measurement** and click **Metric**.
4. Go to **Method** and click **LIM**.
5. Go to **File | Open**. In the message box "Look In," browse to the folder containing the CSV data, and select the file name.

This should successfully import the CSV file onto the **Single/Combined** page of SnagPRO. Although there are three strata for this analysis, each is treated as if it is part of a nonstratified landscape to obtain the information necessary for input onto the Combination page. Therefore, all analyses will be based on the Single/Combined page.

Note that additional columns have been added to your file. The Section and Segment columns were inserted between Transect and Subsegment. SnagPRO combined consecutive subsegments (12.5-m lengths) into segments (25-m lengths), and segments into sections (50-m lengths) to allow for optimal transect length analysis.

Formula entry—

The next step is to have SnagPRO insert the appropriate formula in the Qualify column. This formula determines which logs are included in the current analysis. Begin with all logs ≥15 cm LED. To do this, click on **Volume** under the **Formula** menu on the **Single/Combined** page. Then click on **Set Criteria** button located in the bottom-left of the screen.

To create the correct formula, based on your survey objectives, enter:

1. "15" for LED.
2. "0" for Length (the default when log lengths are not measured).
3. "0" for Condition (the default when log condition is not measured).
4. "9999" for Species (all log species are considered).

SnagPRO evaluates each log by the criteria listed above. For logs meeting all criteria, SnagPRO takes the intersect diameter of each log, squares it, and places this value in the Qualify column. Then SnagPRO inserts these values in the LIM estimator (equation 4a) to obtain volume estimates.

Analyzing by Transect Length—

SnagPRO calculates averages and standard deviations for each transect length within each stratum on the Summary Statistics page. To calculate the statistics for the current forest conditions:

1. Click on the **Summary Statistics** tab.
2. Click on the **Single/Combined** circle in the Analyze Data From section.
3. Click on the **Calculate Statistics** button.

SnagPRO subtotals the values for each transect length (Subsegment_12.5, Segment_25, Section_50, and Transect_100). The number on the end of each label gives the length of the transect in meters. To the right of the subtotaled values are the averages, standard deviations, and current sample sizes for each transect length. These values were simultaneously transferred to the Optimal page.

Optimal transect length—

To determine the transect length that optimizes sampling in current forest conditions, switch to the **Optimal** page. First, write a brief description of the study area and log characteristics in the box labeled **Qualifying Logs**. For example, for this analysis you might write:

Qualifying Logs: Stratum 2; logs ≥15 cm LED; ≥1 m long.

Under the heading **Single/Combined** on the **Optimal** page, notice each transect listed by name and length. The Average column provides the estimated average values (squared intersects multiplied by specific gravity) from the Qualify column for the four transect lengths. Standard deviations for these same values are shown in the next column.

Results under the heading Volume (m³/ha) show that this stand supports about 72.8 m³/ha of logs in this size class of interest (≥15 cm LED; ≥1 m long). Note that the English equivalent is given in the last column (1,041 ft³/ac). The two columns labeled Estimated Sample Size Required and Estimated Total Survey Distance Required, calculate the total number of transect sections and total length of transect, respectively, required to obtain a weight estimate within 20 percent of the true mean 90 percent of the time.

To select the optimal transect length, look at the column Estimated Total Survey Distance Required. In this example, the subsegments, which are 12.5 m long, require the shortest length for sampling (2304 m). By contrast, if 100-m transects are used, 6942 m of transect length would be required. But are subsegments independent? To test for independence:

1. Switch back to the **Summary Statistics** page.
2. Click on the **Correlation** button.
3. Enter "Subsegment" into **Correlation Length** box.

The message box displays the correlation coefficient (r = 0.255) and the coefficient of determination (r² = 0.067). Based on these results, subsegments appear independent and may be used in this analysis.

The last column in section two of the Optimal page is Additional Samples Required. This states how many meters of transect are still required to obtain a precise estimate after taking into account the sampling completed during the pilot survey. For this example, a little over 1300 m additional sampling would be required in stratum 2 to obtain a volume estimate within desired precision.

Volume analysis—

Volume estimates with a bound and precision level are given on the Volume page in SnagPRO. To obtain these values:

1. Click on the **Volume** tab.
2. Click on the **Simple-Random Sampling Equation** tab.
3. Click the **Single** button under the **Calculate** heading.

Results indicate that this stand supports an estimated 72.8 ± 22.1 m³/ha of logs in this size class. (Recall that the precision of an estimate is calculated by dividing the bound by the mean.) In this example, the estimated precision is 30.4 percent, which can be interpreted as being 90 percent confident that the volume estimate in stratum 2 is within 30.4 percent of the true volume. At this point, a decision must be made as to whether the estimate is precise enough to meet management objectives, or whether to sample along 13 more 100-m transects (as indicated on the Optimal page) to improve the precision within this stratum.

To ensure that accurate numbers are entered onto the Combination page, print the results from the **Volume** page. To do this:

1. From the **File** menu select **Print Preview**.
2. Then choose either **Print Portrait** or **Print Landscape**.
3. Click **Print**.

The next step is to obtain volume estimates of logs ≥25 cm LED. To do this, repeat all steps listed above, starting with the "Formula Entry" section, but when prompted to enter the qualifying LED, enter 25 instead of 15.

On the Optimal page, results indicate that subsegments are the optimal transect length, requiring about 3354 m of transect. Check if these lengths are independent by clicking on the **Correlation** button on the **Summary Statistics** page. Results show that adjacent subsegments for this log size class are independent ($r = 0.17$; $r^2 = 0.029$). Therefore, we will proceed with this length.

On the **Volume** page, click on the **Single** button to have the results from the Optimal page transferred. It is estimated that there are 54.1 ± 19.8 m³/ha of logs in this size class (773 ft³/ac). Precision is 36.6 percent. Print this page to save the statistics for input onto the Combination page.

Stratum 3 analysis—

To obtain volume estimates for stratum 3, import the data by clicking on **File** and directing SnagPRO to the CSV file containing data for stratum 3. Then repeat all instructions for stratum 3, as listed above for stratum 2. Print results from the Volume page for both log size classes when completed.

Based on the results shown on the Optimal page, stratum 3 supports an estimated 145 m^3/ha of logs ≥15 cm LED, or 2,076 ft^3/ac. It appears that the best transect length in stratum 3 is the segment. Using this length requires an estimated 443 m of transect, assuming the segments are independent.

The serial correlation test, however, shows that segments may not be independent (r = 0.45). Values above this level are not considered independent (r = 0.403; r^2 = 0.163). Although we will continue to use this transect length for our analysis, assume for a moment that we want to choose a different length. The next best choice would be subsegments based on the results on the Optimal page. The correlation test on subsegments shows that this length can be considered independent (r = 0.063; r^2 = 0.004). Subsegments, rather than segments, are better sampling units in this case because of the systematic distribution of logs. Segments were likely regularly hitting, or missing, clumps of logs, whereas using subsegments minimized this phenomenon. Note that the optimal transect length identified by SnagPro can be overriden by selecting a different **Optimal Selection** from the **Settings** menu and using the resulting statistics in the analysis.

The Volume page shows that stratum 3 supports an estimated 145 ± 19.3 m^3/ha. In addition, because log volume was consistently high throughout the stands, with low variability, the precision for this size class, 13.3 percent, has exceeded the desired level. Print the results on the Volume page for use on the Combination page.

Repeating this process for large (≥25 cm LED) logs in stratum 3 shows a volume of 89.1 ± 20.6 m^3/ha. The precision of 23.1 percent is approaching the desired level of 20 percent. Subsegments provide the most precise measurement and can be considered independent (r = 0.187; r^2 = 0.035). Sample size required equals 1334 m of transect length. Print results on the Volume page for use on the Combination page. This completes the analysis with LIM data.

Strip-plot method of analysis—

To obtain SPM volume estimates for stratum 1, import the data into the SPM portion of SnagPRO by using the following steps:

1. Click **Logs** under **Habitat Component**.
2. From the **Method** menu click **SPM**.
3. Click **Yes** to reaffirm a new analysis.

> Subsegments, rather than segments, are better sampling units in this case because of the systematic distribution of logs. Segments were likely regularly hitting, or missing, clumps of logs, whereas using subsegments minimized this phenomenon.

4. Click **Open** in the **File** menu.

5. Direct SnagPRO to the folder where the CSV file containing the SPM data can be found.

This should successfully import the CSV file onto the Single/Combined page of SnagPRO. Note that the Section and Segment columns have been added to the file, inserted between Transect and Subsegment. Also note that although information about endpoints (for density estimates) were not collected, a column labeled Endpoint appears on the data sheet. This formatting is necessary for SnagPRO to work properly.

Formula entry—

The next step is to have SnagPRO insert the appropriate formula in the Qualify column for stratum 1. This formula determines which logs are included in the current analysis. To do this:

1. From the **Formula** menu, select **Volume**.

2. "10" for LED.

3. "0" for EstimLength because you want all logs to be included and only logs ≥1 m long were measured.

4. "3" for Condition (all decay classes considered).

5. "9999" for Species (all log species considered).

For logs meeting the above criteria, SnagPRO calculates the volume of each portion of the log contained within the plot. This value is placed in the Qualify column.

Analyzing by transect length—

SnagPRO calculates averages and standard deviations for each transect length within each stratum on the **Summary Statistics** page. To calculate the statistics for stratum 1:

1. Click on the **Summary Statistics** page.

2. Click on the **Single/Combined** circle in the Analyze Data From section.

3. Click on the **Calculate Statistics** button.

Optimal transect length—

Switch to the Optimal page and write a brief description of the stratum and size class of log being analyzed. For example:

Qualifying Logs: Stratum 1; SPM; logs ≥15 cm LED; ≥1 m long.

The results in the Volume (m^3/ha) column show that this stand supports about 39.3 m^3/ha (562 ft^3/ac) of logs (≥15 cm LED and ≥1 m long). Segments appear to be the best choice for transect length, requiring an estimated 3254 m. Results of the serial correlation test, shown on the Summary Statistics page, indicate that adjacent segments are independent (r = 0.126; r^2 = 0.016).

Volume analysis—

Once the **Volume** page is activated, enter the area of stratum 1 (812) in the box labeled "Landscape Area." Results show that stratum 1 contains an estimated 39.3 ± 14.2 m³/ha. Precision is 36.1 percent. Print the results on the Volume page for use on the Combination page at the end.

Results for large (≥25 cm LED) logs in stratum 1, using the same analytical process, yields a volume of 33.8 ± 14 m³/ha. Precision is 41.4 percent. Segments provide the most precise measurement and are independent (r = 0.134; r^2 = 0.018). Estimated sample size required equals 4270 m. Print the results on the Volume page for use on the Combination page.

Stratified volume analysis—

To obtain a stratified volume estimate using both the LIM and SPM sampling methods, the statistics expressed in a per-unit basis from each Volume page generated above, must be entered onto the Combination page. To do this:

1. Click on **Combination** from the **Method** menu.
2. Click **Yes** to change the method.
3. Click **Volume** from the **Formula** menu.

There are two sheets available on the Combination page. Shaded boxes require input from users. The **Parameter Estimate** page (fig. 18) uses a stratified-random sampling equation to calculate a mean, bound, and precision for measurements expressed in a per-unit basis (hectares or acres). The Sample Sizes page provides the Estimated Sample Size Required for estimates expressed in hectares or acres.

Follow these steps to obtain an estimate of log volume (≥15 cm LED) for the entire subwatershed using the results printed out for each stratum:

1. Enter the numbers "1," "2," and "3" under the heading Stratum.
2. Under the heading Transect Section Names select **Segment, Subsegment,** and **Segment** from the drop-down menu for strata 1, 2, and 3, respectively.
3. Enter the numbers "812," "654," and "490" for number of hectares in strata 1, 2, and 3, respectively.
4. Enter the estimated volume of logs per hectare for each strata under the heading Parameter Estimates. For strata 1, 2, and 3 there were 39.3, 72.8, and 145 m³/ha, respectively.
5. Enter the estimated variance for strata 1, 2, and 3. These values were 2884, 14,027, and 5,370, respectively.
6. Enter the number of samples for each stratum. This should be 40, 80, and 40 for strata 1, 2, and 3, respectively.

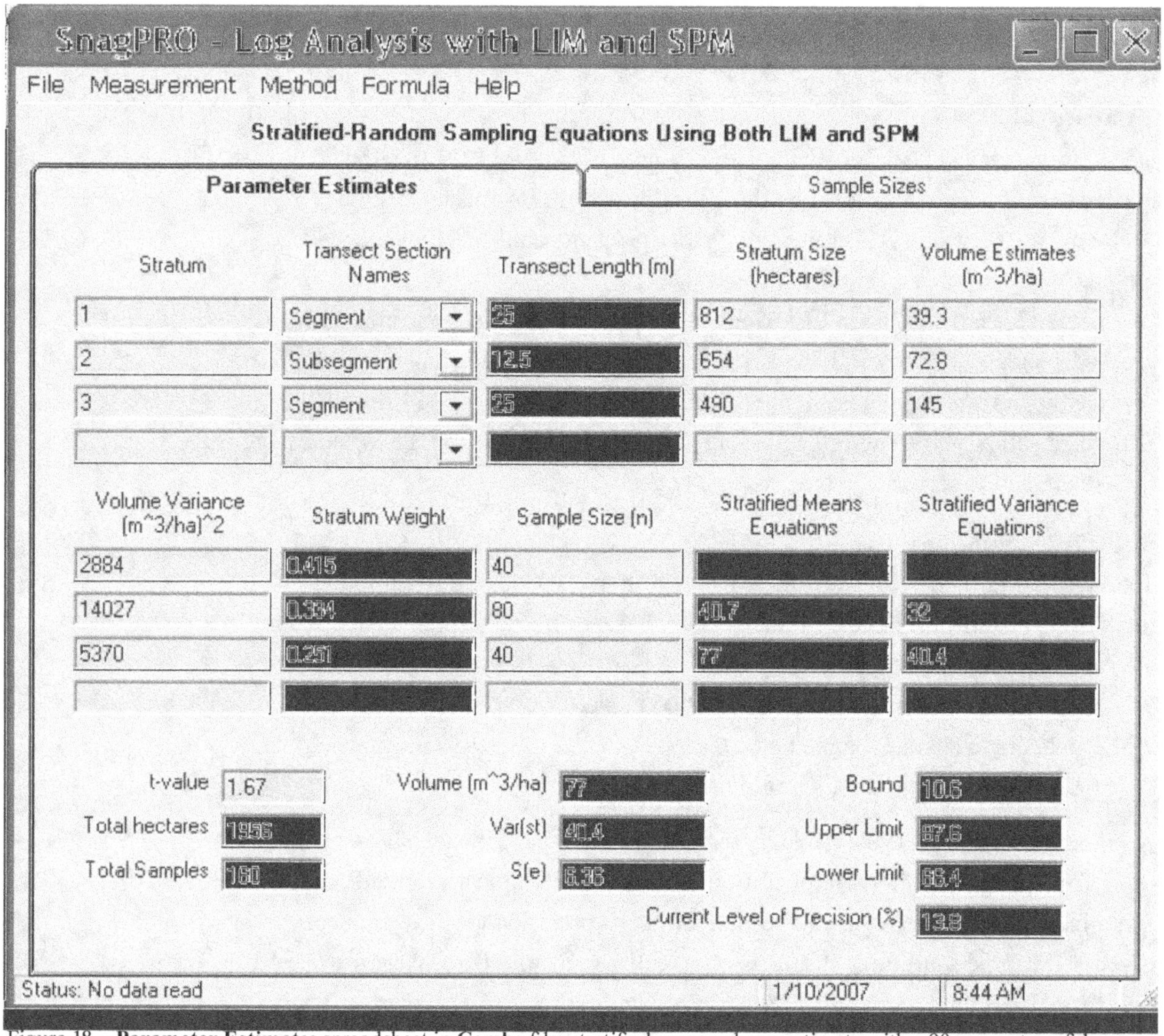

Figure 18—**Parameter Estimates** spreadsheet in **Combo** file: stratified mean volume estimate with a 90-percent confidence interval for qualifying logs. Data are from Tutorial III using line-intersect method (LIM) for one stratum and strip-plot method (SPM) for another.

The stratified volume estimate for this subwatershed is 77 ± 10.6 m³/ha with a precision of 13.8 percent (fig. 18). Repeating this process for large logs yields a stratified volume estimate of 54.4 ± 10.2 m³/ha with a precision of 19 percent.

Conclusions for multiple strata using a combination of LIM and SPM—
Although the estimates of log volume within strata 1 and 2 were not as precise as desired (were not <20 percent), the stratified estimates of log volume for the entire subwatershed exceeded the desired precision for logs in both size classes. This suggests that both the sampling design and stratification process for this subwatershed worked well to meet objectives.

As shown by these Tutorials, SnagPro offers a variety of analysis procedures geared to meet different management objectives. Key analytical steps included in these examples were importing data from an Excel spreadsheet, obtaining a variety of basic metrics on unstratified and stratified data, and use of a pilot sample to estimate the appropriate sample size needed to meet overall survey objectives.

The importance of logs in research and management to meet a variety of resource objectives suggests that methods outlined here are needed as an efficient and accurate way to evaluate log conditions. Supporting SnagPro software provides a process of data entry, management, and analysis that is easy to follow and minimizes analysis mistakes. We urge researchers and managers of logs to consider using these tools to aid in the work on this important resource.

> **The importance of logs in research and management to meet a variety of resource objectives suggests that methods outlined here are needed as an efficient and accurate way to evaluate log conditions.**

Acknowledgments

We thank Ray Davis, Deb Hennessy, Jennifer Weikel, and Christina Vojta for detailed comments on SnagPRO operations and this manuscript. Kim Mellen and Amy Jacobs reviewed earlier versions of our manuscript. Daniel Jones, Jennifer Carpenedo, Gene Paul, Kent Coe, Alexa Michel, Darren Hopkins, Damon Page, Cynthia Sandoval, Eric Sandoz, Lee Stultz, and Peter Barry assisted in data collection. Andrew Youngblood and Kerry Mettlen assisted in obtaining land area measurements. The USDA Forest Service—specifically the Pacific Northwest Research Station and Washington office of National Forest System—provided funding for this project. The Flathead National Forest in Montana provided equipment and consultation. We also thank James Brown and Tim Max for their assistance with sampling methods pertaining to the line-intersect method. Kirk Steinhorst provided advice and reviews of statistical methods presented here.

English Equivalents

When you know:	Multiply by:	To find:
Centimeters (cm)	0.394	Inches (in)
Meters (m)	3.281	Feet (ft)
Square meters (m²)	10.76	Square feet (ft²)
Hectares (ha)	2.471	Acres (ac)
Logs per ha (logs/ha)	.405	Logs per acre (logs/ac)
Meters per ha (m/ha)	1.328	Feet per acre (ft/ac)
Cubic meters per ha (m³/ha)	14.29	Cubic feet per acre (ft³/ac)
Metric tons per ha	.446	English tons per acre
Kilograms per cubic meter (kg/m³)	.0624	Pounds per cubic foot (lb/ft³)

References

Bartels, R.; Dell, J.D.; Knight, R.L.; Schaefer, G. 1985. Dead and down woody material. In: Brown, E.R., tech. ed. Management of wildlife and fish habitats in forests of western Oregon and Washington. Part 1: Chapter narratives. R-6F&WL-191-1985. Portland, OR: U.S. Department of Agriculture, Forest Service, Pacific Northwest Region: 171–186.

Bate, L.J.; Garton, E.O.; Wisdom, M.J. 1999a. Estimating snag and large tree densities and distributions on a landscape for wildlife management. Gen. Tech. Rep. PNW-GTR-425. Portland, OR: U.S. Department of Agriculture, Forest Service, Pacific Northwest Research Station. 76 p.

Bate, L.J.; Torgersen, T.R.; Garton, E.O.; Wisdom, M.J. 1999b. Estimating the density, total length, and percent cover of logs on a landscape for wildlife management. Unpublished report. On file with: USDA Forest Service, Forestry and Range Sciences Laboratory, 1401 Gekeler Lane, La Grande, OR 97850.

Bate, L.J.; Torgersen, T.R.; Garton, E.O.; Wisdom, M.J. 2004. Performance of two sampling methods to estimate log characteristics for wildlife. Forest Ecology and Management. 199(2004): 83–102.

Bate, L.J.; Wisdom, M.J.; Garton, E.O.; Clabough, S.C. [In press]. SnagPRO: snag and large tree sampling methods and analyses for wildlife. Gen. Tech. Rep. Portland, OR: U.S. Department of Agriculture, Forest Service, Pacific Northwest Research Station.

Bell, G.; Kerr, A.; McNickle, D.; Woollons, R. 1996. Accuracy of the line intersect method of post-logging sampling under orientation bias. Forest Ecology and Management. 84(1996): 23–28.

Brown, J.K. 1974. Handbook for inventorying downed woody material. Gen. Tech. Rep. INT-GTR-16. Ogden, UT: U.S. Department of Agriculture, Forest Service, Intermountain Forest and Range Experiment Station. 24 p.

Brown, J.K.; See, T.E. 1981. Downed dead wood fuel and biomass in the Northern Rocky Mountains. Gen. Tech. Rep. INT-GTR-117. Ogden, UT: U.S. Department of Agriculture, Forest Service, Intermountain Forest and Range Experiment Station. 48 p.

Bull, E.L.; Carter, B.; Henjum, M. [and others]. 1991. Monitoring protocol-October 1991. Protocol for monitoring woodpeckers and snags in the Pacific Northwest region of U.S. Forest Service. Unpublished report. 8 p. On file with: USDA Forest Service, Forestry and Range Sciences Laboratory, 1401 Gekeler Lane, La Grande, OR 97850.

Bull, E.L.; Henjum, M.G. 1990. Ecology of the great gray owl. Gen. Tech. Rep. PNW-GTR-265. Portland, OR: U.S. Department of Agriculture, Forest Service, Pacific Northwest Research Station. 39 p.

Bull, E.L.; Holthausen, R.S. 1993. Habitat use and management of pileated woodpeckers in northeastern Oregon. Journal of Wildlife Management. 57: 335–345.

Bull, E.L.; Parks, C.G.; Torgersen, T.R. 1997. Trees and logs important to wildlife in the interior Columbia River basin. Gen. Tech. Rep. PNW-GTR-391. Portland, OR: U.S. Department of Agriculture, Forest Service, Pacific Northwest Research Station. 55 p.

Bull, E.L.; Torgersen, T.R.; Wertz, T.L. 2001. The importance of vegetation, insects, and neonate ungulates in black bear diet in northeastern Oregon. Northwest Science. 75: 244–253.

Carey, A.B.; Johnson, M.L. 1995. Small mammals in managed, unharvested young, and old-growth forests. Ecological Applications. 5: 336–352.

Cochran, W.G. 1977. Sampling techniques. 3rd ed. New York: John Wiley and Sons. 428 p.

De Vries, P.G. 1973. A general theory on line intersect sampling with application to logging residue inventory. Wageningen, The Netherlands: Mededelingen Landbouwhogeschool 73–11. 23 p.

Franklin, J.F.; Cromack, K., Jr.; Denison, W. [and others]. 1981. Ecological characteristics of old-growth Douglas-fir forests. Gen. Tech. Rep. PNW-118. Portland, OR: U.S. Department of Agriculture, Forest Service, Pacific Northwest Forest and Range Experiment Station. 48 p.

Fischer, W.C. 1981. Photo guide for appraising downed woody fuels in Montana forests: grand fir-larch-Douglas-fir, western hemlock, western hemlock-western redcedar, and western redcedar cover types. Gen. Tech. Rep. INT-96. Ogden, UT: U.S. Department of Agriculture, Forest Service, Intermountain Forest and Range Experiment Station. 53 p.

Harmon, M.E.; Franklin, J.F.; Swanson, F.J. [and others]. 1986. Ecology of coarse woody debris in temperate ecosystems. Advances in Ecological Research. 15: 133–302.

Harvey, A.E.; Jurgensen, M.F.; Larsen, M.J.; Graham, R.T. 1987. Decaying organic materials and soil quality in the inland Northwest: a management opportunity. Gen. Tech. Rep. INT-GTR-225. Ogden, UT: U.S. Department of Agriculture, Forest Service, Intermountain Forest and Range Experiment Station. 15 p.

Hayes, J.P.; Cross, S.P. 1987. Characteristics of logs used by western red-backed voles and deer mice. Canadian Field Naturalist. 101: 543–546.

Hazard, J.W.; Pickford, S.G. 1978. Simulation studies on line intercept sampling of forest residue. Forest Science. 24: 469–483.

Hazard, J.W.; Pickford, S.G. 1986. Simulation studies on line intersect sampling of forest residue, Part II. Forest Science. 32: 447–470.

Hurlbert, S.H. 1984. Pseudoreplication and the design of ecological field experiments. Ecological Monographs. 54(2): 187–211.

Husch, B.; Miller, C.I.; Beers, T.W. 1972. Forest mensuration. 2nd ed. New York: Ronald Press Company. 410 p.

Jurgensen, M.F.; Harvey, A.E.; Graham, R.T. [and others]. 1997. Impacts of timber harvesting on soil organic matter, nitrogen, productivity, and health of inland Northwest forests. Forest Science. 43: 234–251.

Koehler, G.M.; Aubry, K.B. 1994. Lynx. In: Ruggiero, L.F.; Aubry, K.B.; Buskirk, S.W. [and others], tech. eds. The scientific basis for conserving forest carnivores. Gen. Tech. Rep. RM-GTR-254. Fort Collins, CO: U.S. Department of Agriculture, Forest Service, Rocky Mountain Forest and Range Experiment Station: 74–98.

Krebs, C.J. 1989. Ecological methodology. New York: Harper Collins Publishers, Inc. 654 p.

Lofroth, E. 1998. The dead wood cycle. In: Voller, J.; Harrison, S., eds. Conservation biology principles for forested landscapes. Vancouver, BC: UBC Press: 185–214.

Maser, C.; Anderson, R.G.; Ralph, G. [and others]. 1979. Dead and down woody material. In: Thomas, J.W., tech. ed. Wildlife habitats in managed forests—the Blue Mountains of Oregon and Washington. Agric. Handb. 533. Washington, DC: U.S. Department of Agriculture, Forest Service: 78–95.

Mellen, K.; Marcot, B.G.; Ohmann, J.L. [and others]. 2006. DecAID, the decayed wood advisor for managing snags, partially dead trees, and down wood for biodiversity in forests of Washington and Oregon. Version 2.0. Portland, OR: U.S. Department of Agriculture, Forest Service, Pacific Northwest Region and Pacific Northwest Research Station; U.S. Department of the Interior, Fish and Wildlife Service, Oregon State Office. http://wwwnotes.fs.fed.us:81/pnw/ DecAID/DecAID.nsf. (19 December 2007).

Norris, L.A. 1990. An overview and synthesis of knowledge concerning natural and prescribed fire in the Pacific Northwest forest. In: Walstad, J.D.; Radosevich, S.R.; Sandberg, D.V., eds. Natural and prescribed fire in Pacific Northwest forests. Corvallis, OR: Oregon State University Press: 7–22. Chapter 2.

Powell, R.A.; Zielinski, W.J. 1994. Fisher. In: Ruggiero, L.F.; Aubry, K.B; Buskirk, S.W. [and others], tech. eds. The scientific basis for conserving forest carnivores. Gen. Tech. Rep. RM-GTR-254. Fort Collins, CO: U.S. Department of Agriculture, Forest Service, Rocky Mountain Forest and Range Experiment Station: 38–73.

Quigley, T.M.; Haynes, R.W.; Graham, R.T., tech. eds. 1996. Integrated scientific assessment for ecosystem management in the interior Columbia basin and portions of the Klamath and Great Basins. Gen. Tech. Rep. PNW-GTR-382. Portland, OR: U.S. Department of Agriculture, Forest Service, Pacific Northwest Research Station. 303 p.

Sandberg, D.V.; Ottmar, R.D. 1983. Slash burning and fuel consumption in the Douglas-fir subregion. In: Proceedings of the 7th American Meteorological Society and Society of American Foresters conference on fire and forest meteorology. Boston, MA: American Meteorological Society: 90–93.

Sheehan, K.A. 1996. Effects of insecticide treatments on subsequent defoliation by western spruce budworm in Oregon and Washington: 1982-92. Gen. Tech. Rep. PNW-GTR-367. Portland, OR: U.S. Department of Agriculture, Forest Service, Pacific Northwest Research Station. 55 p.

Sokal, R.R.; Rohlf, F.J. 1981. Biometry. New York: W.H. Freeman and Company. 859 p.

Swihart, R.K.; Slade, N.A. 1985. Testing for independence of observations in animal movements. Ecology. 66(4): 1176–1184.

Tallmon, D.; Mills, S. 1994. Use of logs within home ranges of California red-backed voles on a remnant of forest. Journal of Mammalogy. 75: 97–101.

Torgersen, T.R.; Bull, E.L. 1995. Down logs as habitat for forest-dwelling ants—the primary prey of pileated woodpeckers in northeastern Oregon. Northwest Science. 69: 294–303.

U.S. Department of Agriculture, Forest Service. 1991. Field procedures guide: stand examination program. Portland, OR: Pacific Northwest Region. 62 p.

U.S. Department of Agriculture, Forest Service. 1995. Flathead National Forest Plan. Kalispell, MT. 555 p.

Walstad, J.D.; Radosevich, S.R.; Sandberg, D.V. 1990. Natural and prescribed fire in Pacific Northwest forests. Corvallis, OR: Oregon State University Press. 317 p.

Warren, W.G.; Olsen, P.F. 1964. A line intersect technique for assessing logging waste. Forest Science. 10(3): 267-276.

Zar, J.H. 1984. Biostatistical analysis. Englewood Cliffs, NJ: Prentice-Hall, Inc. 718 p.

Appendix 1: Customized Log Measuring Sticks

We recommend buying calipers for log surveys, but realize that the investment in calipers to measure log diameters may make log sampling cost prohibitive. Although not as accurate as calipers, customized log measuring sticks provide an economical and efficient alternative. The stick consists of three parts: (1) straight rule on one side, (2) graduated rule on opposite side, and (3) square. The straight-ruled side is for measuring log lengths within the strip plots. The graduated rule is a Biltmore stick, which gives diameter measurements. Finally, the square is useful to help determine the outer boundaries of the plots used in the strip-plot method (SPM) (fig. 2a and 2b). The figure below illustrates the design and construction using a hardwood with metric measurements. For English measurement users, the measuring stick should be 3 ft long.

Biltmore sticks should be held 63.5 cm (25 in) from the eyes. This can be customized, however, to meet the needs of the user. Closing one eye, line up the zero end of the stick with one side of the tree. Both the straight and graduated rules should begin at the far side of the stick. Then shift the same eye, while maintaining the position of your head, to read where the opposite side of the tree intersects the Biltmore graduations. The place where the two intersect, indicates the diameter of the log.

The graduations for creating the Biltmore side of the stick can be found by the following equation (Husch and others 1972):

$$B = \frac{D}{\sqrt{1 + \dfrac{D}{E}}}$$

where
B = distance from zero point of the stick to the position for a given diameter,
D = log diameter, and
E = perpendicular distance from eye to stick.

81

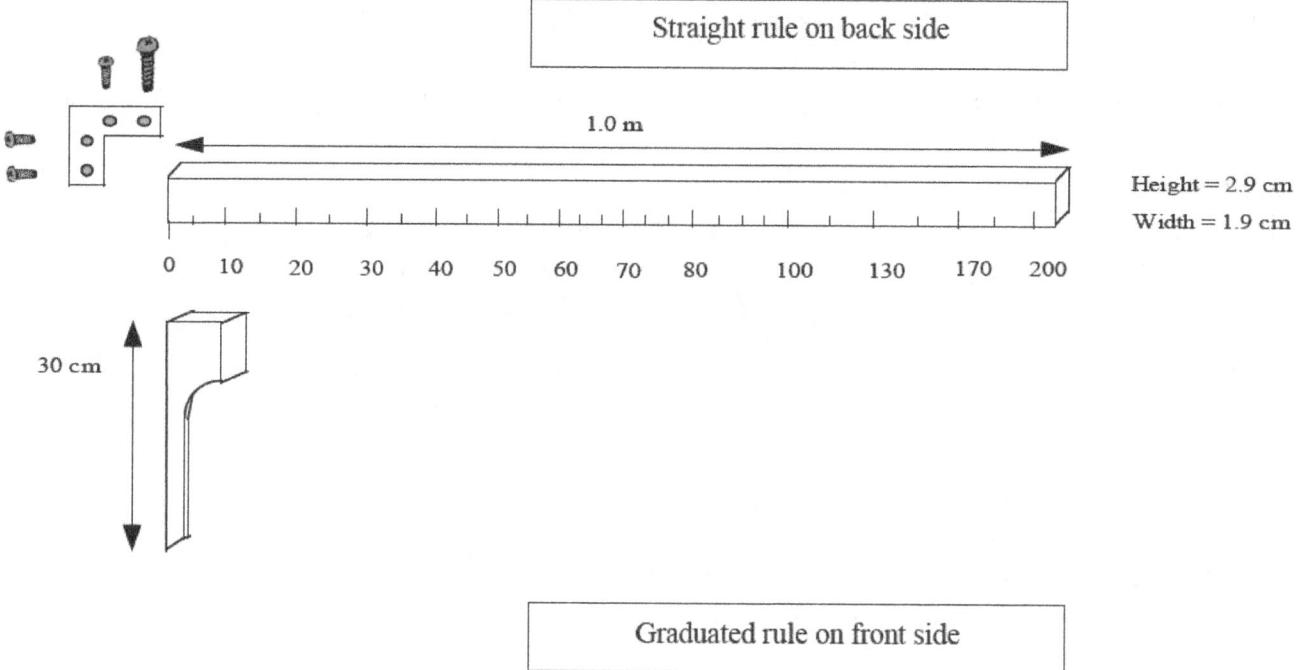

Straight rule on back side

1.0 m

Height = 2.9 cm

Width = 1.9 cm

0   10   20   30   40   50   60   70   80   100   130   170   200

30 cm

Graduated rule on front side

Appendix 2: Line-Intersect Method (LIM) Field Form Explanations

Example of log definition:

For the purposes of this study, a "log" is defined as any down wood piece whose large-end diameter (LED) is >7.6 cm (3 in). A log qualifies if its central axis (the center of the bole or the pith) is intersected by the transect line (fig. 3). Its axis must lie above the ground (above duff and mineral soil layer). Dead stems attached to a live tree are not counted. Multiple branches attached to dead trees or shrubs are each tallied separately. For leaning dead trees, if the angle between the dead tree and the ground is <45 degrees it is a log; if greater, it is a snag. If the central axis of a suspended log is <1.8 m above the ground where the transect passes, tally the log on the transect; otherwise, disregard it.

1. Stratum: Enter the stratum number: 1, 2, 3, or 4.

2. Location: Enter the stand number in which the plot is contained.

3. Transect: Assign a unique numeric identifier to indicate which 100-m or 400-ft transect is being surveyed (e.g., 1, 2, 3, or 4). No two transects within a survey area should be the same regardless of the stratum.

4. Subsegment: Assign a unique numeric identifier (1 through 8) to indicate which 12.5-m (or 50-ft) subsegment is being surveyed. **Most importantly,** the first subsegment of each transect should start with "1." This will allow SnagPRO to correctly join consecutive subsegments.

5. Species: SnagPRO can accommodate either alpha (six characters) or numeric data. Listed below are the standardized species codes taken from the stand exam program in the Pacific Northwest Region [USDA Forest Service 1991]. Customize for your own use.

Douglas-fir/redwoods:

Douglas-fir (*Pseudotsuga menziesii* (Mirb.) Franco)	202
Redwood (*Sequoia sempervirens* (D. Don) Endl.)	211

True firs:

Pacific silver fir (*Abies amabilis* Dougl. ex Forbes)	011
White fir (*Abies concolor* (Gord. & Glend.) Lindl. ex Hildebr.)	015
Grand fir (*Abies grandis* (Dougl. ex D. Don) Lindl.)	017
Subalpine fir (*Abies lasiocarpa* (Hook.) Nutt.)	019
California red fir (*Abies magnifica* A. Murray var. *magnifica* A. Murray)	020
Shasta red fir (*Abies magnifica* A. Murray var. *shastensis* Lemmon)	021
Noble fir (*Abies procera* Rehd.)	022

Cedars:

Port Orford cedar (*Chamaecyparis lawsoniana* (A. Murr.) Parl.)   041

Alaska cedar (*Chamaecyparis nootkatensis* (D. Don) Spach)   042

Incense-cedar (*Calocedrus decurrens* (Torr.) Florin)   081

Western redcedar (*Thuja plicata* Donn ex D. Don)   242

Larch:

Western larch (*Larix occidentalis* Nutt.)   073

Spruce:

Brewer spruce (*Picea breweriana* Wats.)   092

Englemann spruce (*Picea engelmannii* Parry ex Englm.)   093

Sitka spruce (*Picea sitchensis* (Bong.) Carr.)   098

Pines:

Lodgepole pine (*Pinus contorta* Dougl. ex Loud.)   108

Jeffrey pine (*Pinus jeffreyi* Grev. & Balf.)   116

Sugar pine (*Pinus lambertiana* Dougl.)   117

Western white pine (*Pinus monticola* Dougl. ex D. Don)   119

Ponderosa pine (*Pinus ponderosa* Dougl. ex Laws.)   122

Hemlock:

Western hemlock (*Tsuga heterophylla* (Raf.) Sarg.)   263

Mountain hemlock (*Tsuga mertensiana* (Bong.) Carr.)   264

Hardwoods:

Bigleaf maple (*Acer macrophyllum* Pursh)   312

Red alder (*Alnus rubra* Bong.)   351

Western paper birch (*Betula papyrifera* Marsh.)   376

Pacific madrone (*Arbutus menziesii* Pursh)   361

Golden chinkapin (*Castanopsis chrysophylla* (Dougl.) A. DC)   431

Oregon ash (*Fraxinus latifolia* Benth.)   542

Tanoak (*Lithocarpus densiflorus* (Hook. & Arn.) Rehd.)   631

Quaking aspen (*Populus tremuloides* Michx.)   746

Black cottonwood (*Populus trichocarpa* Torr. & Gray)   747

Oregon white oak (*Quercus garryana* Dougl. ex Hook.)   815

California black oak (*Quercus kelloggii* Newb.)   818

Oregon myrtle (*Umbellularia californica* (Hook. & Arn.) Nutt.)   981

Other conifers:

Subalpine larch (*Larix lyallii* Parl.)	072
Cypress (*Cupressus*)	050
All junipers (*Juniperus*)	060
Pacific yew (*Taxus brevifolia* Nutt.)	231
Knobcone pine (*Pinus attenuate* Lemm.)	103
Limber pine (*Pinus flexilis* James)	113
Whitebark pine (*Pinus albicaulis* Engelm.)	101

6. Intersect: Enter the diameter (cm or in) of the qualifying log at the point where the transect intersects the log (fig. 3).

7. LED: Enter the LED in centimeters (in) of the qualifying log that is intersected. If roots are still attached, measure the LED just above the butt swell where the breast height would occur if the tree were still standing (fig. 5). This is important: If no logs are encountered along the entire length of the subsegment, enter "9999" in the LED space.

8. Condition: Enter the numeric value (1 or 2) for the corresponding decay class (hard or soft) of the log encountered. See Maser and others (1979) and Bull and others (1997) for more detailed decay classes and definitions that also can be used.
    1= Sound (hard, would burn for awhile)
    2= Rotten (decayed, not much fuel value)

9. Length: (Optional) Enter the total length of the log including the rootwad, if present. Measure out to where the small-end diameter is 2.5 cm or 1 in (fig. 1a).

Appendix 3: Split-Plot Method (SPM) Field Form Explanations

Example of log definition:

For the purposes of this study, a log is defined as any down woody piece with a large-end diameter (LED) >23 cm (9 in) and >1 m (39 in) in length. To be counted, >0.1 m (4 in) length of a log must be contained within the plot (fig. 1). For logs broken into two pieces, treat them as one log if the pieces are touching. Otherwise, treat them as separate logs. Its axis must lie above the ground (above duff and mineral soil layer). Dead stems attached to a live tree are not counted. Multiple branches attached to dead trees or shrubs are each tallied separately. For leaning dead trees, if the angle between the dead tree and the ground is <45 degrees, it is a log; if greater, it is a snag. If the central axis of a suspended log is >1.8 m (6 ft) above the ground within the strip plot, disregard it.

1. Stratum: Enter the stratum number: 1, 2, 3, or 4.

2. Location: Enter the stand number in which the plot is contained.

3. Transect: Assign a unique numeric identifier to indicate which 100-m or 400-ft transect is being surveyed (e.g., 1, 2, 3, or 4). No two transects should be the same regardless of the stratum.

4. Subsegment: Assign a unique numeric identifier (1 through 8) to indicate which subsegment is being surveyed. **Most importantly**, the first subsegment of each transect should start with "1." This will allow SnagPRO to correctly join consecutive subsegments.

5. LED: Enter the LED of the qualifying log, regardless if it falls in or out of the boundaries of the strip plot, to the nearest centimeter or inch. If roots are still attached, measure the LED just above the butt swell where breast height would occur if the tree were still standing (fig. 5). Otherwise, measure diameter at largest point where log is still intact. This is important: enter the number "9999" if no logs were contained within this plot.

6. Endpoint: For each qualifying log whose endpoint (LED) falls within the boundaries of the plot, enter "1"; otherwise, enter "0." If density is the only parameter of interest, simply conduct a tally of logs whose endpoints are contained within the strip plot boundaries. If no endpoints are contained within a subsegment, record "9999" in the LED column and "0" in the Endpoint column.

7. Large: For logs within the plot boundaries, enter the diameter (cm or in) of the log at its large end (see fig. 1b).

8. Small: For logs within the plot boundaries, enter the diameter (cm or in) of the log at its smallest end (fig. 1b).

9. Length: If the entire log lies within the bounds of the plot, enter the length of the log between the small- and large-end diameters (fig. 1b). Otherwise, measure the length of the log that lies within the plot (fig. 9). Length measurements should not extend past 2 m (6 ft) from the centerline. The 2 m (6 ft) distance is the perpendicular distance along the ground between the centerline transect and the central axis (pith) of the log.

10. Condition: Enter the numeric value for the corresponding decay class (hard or soft) of the log encountered. See Maser and others (1979) and Bull and others (1997) for more detailed decay classes and definitions that also can be used.

    1 = Sound (hard, would burn for awhile)

    2 = Rotten (decayed, not much fuel value)

11. Use: Enter the appropriate code to indicate whether or not the log displays wildlife signs. This should be customized for the species of interest.

    0 = None observed

    1 = Wildlife signs (e.g., woodpecker foraging, bear foraging, squirrel middens, other).

12. Species: SnagPRO can accommodate either alpha (six characters) or numeric data. Listed below are the standardized species codes taken from the Pacific Northwest Region stand exam program in (USDA Forest Service 1991). Customize for your own use.

Douglas-fir/redwoods:

Douglas-fir (*Pseudotsuga menziesii* (Mirb.) Franco)	202
Redwood (*Sequoia sempervirens* (D. Don) Endl.)	211

True firs:

Pacific silver fir (*Abies amabilis* Dougl. ex Forbes)	011
White fir (*Abies concolor* (Gord. & Glend.) Lindl. ex Hildebr.)	015
Grand fir (*Abies grandis* (Dougl. ex D. Don) Lindl.)	017
Subalpine fir (*Abies lasiocarpa* (Hook.) Nutt.)	019
California red fir (*Abies magnifica* A. Murray var. *magnifica* A. Murray)	020
Shasta red fir (*Abies magnifica* A. Murray var. *shastensis* Lemmon)	021
Noble fir (*Abies procera* Rehd.)	022

Cedars:

Port Orford cedar (*Chamaecyparis lawsoniana* (A. Murr.) Parl.)	041
Alaska cedar (*Chamaecyparis nootkatensis* (D. Don) Spach)	042
Incense-cedar (*Calocedrus decurrens* (Torr.) Florin)	081
Western redcedar (*Thuja plicata* Donn ex D. Don)	242

Larch:

Western larch (*Larix occidentalis* Nutt.) 073

Spruce:

Brewer spruce (*Picea breweriana* Wats.) 092

Englemann spruce (*Picea engelmannii* Parry ex Englm.) 093

Sitka spruce (*Picea sitchensis* (Bong.) Carr.) 098

Pines:

Lodgepole pine (*Pinus contorta* Dougl. ex Loud.) 108

Jeffrey pine (*Pinus jeffreyi* Grev. & Balf.) 116

Sugar pine (*Pinus lambertiana* Dougl.) 117

Western white pine (*Pinus monticola* Dougl. ex D. Don) 119

Ponderosa pine (*Pinus ponderosa* Dougl. ex Laws.) 122

Hemlock:

Western hemlock (*Tsuga heterophylla* (Raf.) Sarg.) 263

Mountain hemlock (*Tsuga mertensiana* (Bong.) Carr.) 264

Hardwoods:

Bigleaf maple (*Acer macrophyllum* Pursh) 312

Red alder (*Alnus rubra* Bong.) 351

Western paper birch (*Betula papyrifera* Marsh.) 376

Pacific madrone (*Arbutus menziesii* Pursh) 361

Golden chinkapin (*Castanopsis chrysophylla* (Dougl.) A. DC) 431

Oregon ash (*Fraxinus latifolia* Benth.) 542

Tanoak (*Lithocarpus densiflorus* (Hook. & Arn.) Rehd.) 631

Quaking aspen (*Populus tremuloides* Michx.) 746

Black cottonwood (*Populus trichocarpa* Torr. & Gray) 747

Oregon white oak (*Quercus garryana* Dougl. ex Hook.) 815

California black oak (*Quercus kelloggii* Newb.) 818

Oregon myrtle (*Umbellularia californica* (Hook. & Arn.) Nutt.) 981

Other conifers:

Subalpine larch (*Larix lyallii* Parl.) 072

Cypress (*Cupressus*) 050

All junipers (*Juniperus*) 060

Pacific yew (*Taxus brevifolia* Nutt.) 231

Knobcone pine (*Pinus attenuata* Lemm.) 103

Limber pine (*Pinus flexilis* James) 113

Whitebark pine (*Pinus albicaulis* Engelm.) 101

13. % Length (optional)

Enter the number that best describes what percentage of the log length is contained within the strip plot boundary:

<10%
20%
30%
40%
50%
60%
70%
80%
90%
100%

Appendix 4: General Instructions for Analysis Within a Single Stratum

1. To get started
   a. Double click on SnagPRO.exe.
   b. Click on the **Logs** button under **Habitat Component**.
   c. From the **Measurement** menu, select **Metric** or **English**.
   d. From the **Method** menu select the sampling method: **LIM** or **SPM**.
   e. From the **Formula** menu select the variable of interest: **Density, Length, Percent Cover, Tally, Volume,** or **Weight**.
   f. Open your data file by clicking on **Open** under the **File** menu.
   g. Highlight the name of your CSV file and click **Open**.

2. To set criteria
   a. Single click on tab labeled **Single/Combined**.
   b. Notice segment and section field names have been added and computed for each column.
   c. Click on button in bottom left of screen labeled **Set Criteria**.
   d. Enter minimum LED in message box labeled **LED**.
   e. Enter minimum length of logs to be considered in message box labeled **Length**. Enter "0" if all lengths will be considered or log lengths were not measured.
   f. Enter maximum value for condition class (or decay class) in message box labeled **Condition** (this box does not appear when calculating weight estimates).
   g. Enter numeric code of log species you would like to exclude in box labeled **Species**.

3. Calculate statistics
   a. Click on tab for page labeled **Summarize Statistics**.
   b. On Summarize Statistics page, under Analyze Data From, click on **Single/Combined**.
   c. Then click the **Calculate Statistics** button found directly below.
   d. Click on **Optimal** tab.
   e. Check desired level of precision and t-value; if different values are desired, enter them and repeat steps 3a through 3d.
   f. Enter brief description of stratum and log characteristics for your records.
   g. Examine Optimal page for statistics, estimated sample size required, additional samples required, and optimal transect length.
   h. Run serial correlation analysis for selected plot size.

    i. Print copy of page if desired by selecting **Print Preview** from the **File** menu, then clicking tab labeled **Print**.

4. Variable estimate

    a. Click on tab with the name of the variable of interest: **Density, Length, Percent Cover, Tally, Volume,** or **Weight.**

    b. Check to ensure t-value is correct for the analysis.

    c. Select tab labeled **Simple-Random Sampling Equation.**

    d. For SPM analyses, enter landscape area (hectares or acres).

    e. Under **Calculate** heading click tab labeled **Single**.

    f. Examine variable sheet for estimated parameters and current level of precision to decide whether an adequate number of samples have been taken. Refer back to the Optimal page for additional number of samples to take to reach desired level of precision.

5. Statistical test

    a. Enter the target value of the variable you are testing.

    b. Enter the estimated value of the variable you are testing.

    c. Enter the bound.

    d. If target value (red line) falls within the bounds (green lines) of the estimated value (blue line), accept the null hypothesis: There is no difference between the estimated and target values for the given variable; otherwise, reject the null hypothesis.

    e. For borderline cases, consider additional sampling effort.

Appendix 5: General Instructions for Analysis Within a Stratified Landscape

1. To get started
   a. Double click on SnagPRO.exe.
   b. Click on the **Logs** button under **Habitat Component**.
   c. From the **Measurement** menu, select **Metric** or **English**.
   d. From the **Method** menu select the sampling method: **LIM** or **SPM**.
   e. From the **Formula** menu select the variable of interest: **Density, Length, Percent Cover, Tally, Volume,** or **Weight.**
   f. Open your data file by clicking on **Open** under the **File** menu.
   g. Highlight the name of your CSV file and click **Open**.
   h. Notice that segment and section field names have been added and computed for each column.

2. To set criteria to all strata
   a. Click on tab labeled **Stratum 1**.
   b. Click on the **Apply and Sort** button.
   c. Enter minimum LED in message box labeled **LED**.
   d. Enter minimum length of logs to be considered in message box labeled **Length**. Enter "0" if all lengths will be considered or log lengths were not measured.
   e. Enter maximum value for condition class (or decay class) in message box labeled **Condition** (this box does not appear when calculating weight estimates).
   f. Enter numeric code of log species you would like to exclude in box labeled **Species**.

3. Calculate statistics
   a. Click on **Summarize Statistics** page.
   b. On Summarize Statistics page, under heading "Analyze Data From," click on **Stratum 1**.
   c. Then click the **Calculate Statistics** button found directly below.
   d. Repeat 3b and 3c for each stratum.
   e. Click on page labeled **Optimal**.
   f. Check desired level of precision and t-value; if different values are desired, enter them and repeat steps 3a through 3d.
   g. Enter brief description of stratum and log characteristics for your records.
   h. Examine Optimal page for statistics, estimated sample size required, additional samples required, and optimal transect length for stratum 1.

    i. Run serial correlation analysis for selected plot size.

    j. Print copy of page if desired by selecting **Print Preview** from the **File** menu, then clicking tab labeled **Print**.

    k. Repeat 3g through 3i for all strata.

4. Variable estimate

    a. Click on tab with the name of the variable of interest: **Density, Length, Percent Cover, Tally, Volume,** or **Weight.**

    b. Check to ensure t-value is correct for the analysis.

    c. Select tab labeled **Stratified-Random Sampling Equation**.

    d. Enter the correct stratum size (in hectares or acres) in each of the input boxes that corresponds to the number of strata in your analysis at the bottom of the page; otherwise, leave blank.

    e. Under **Calculate** heading click the **Stratified** tab.

    f. Examine variable sheet for estimated parameters and current level of precision.

5. Sample size required

    a. Click on page labeled **Sample Size**.

    b. Examine Optimal and Proportional sections for estimated sample sizes required within each stratum. Refer to the "Parameter Estimates for a Stratified Landscape" section on differences between the two allocation methods.

6. Statistical test

    a. Click on **Statistical Test** page.

    b. Enter the target value of the variable you are testing.

    c. Enter the estimated value of the variable you are testing.

    d. Enter its bound.

    e. If target value (red line) falls within the bounds (green lines) of the estimated value (blue line), accept the null hypothesis: There is no difference between the estimated and target values for the given variable; otherwise, reject the null hypothesis.

    f. For borderline cases, consider additional sampling effort.

www.ingramcontent.com/pod-product-compliance
Lightning Source LLC
Chambersburg PA
CBHW080315290526

45790CB00005B/2054